CLARENCE DAY'S
LIFE WITH FATHER

MADE INTO THREE ACTS
**BY HOWARD LINDSAY
AND RUSSEL CROUSE**

★

DRAMATISTS
PLAY SERVICE
INC.

OSCAR SERLIN presented *LIFE WITH FATHER* at the Maryland Theatre, Baltimore, Maryland, October 30th, 1939 and Empire Theatre, New York, N.Y., November 8th, 1939 with the following cast:

FATHER . . . . Howard Lindsay

VINNIE . . . . Dorothy Stickney

CLARENCE . . . . John Drew Devereaux

JOHN . . . . Richard Simon

WHITNEY . . . . Raymond Roe

HARLAN . . . . Larry Robinson

CORA . . . . Ruth Hammond

MARY SKINNER . . . . Teresa Wright

REV. DR. LLOYD . . . . Richard Sterling

DR. HUMPHREYS . . . . A. H. Van Buren

DR. SOMERS . . . . John C. King

MARGARET . . . . Dorothy Bernard

ANNIE . . . . Katharine Bard

DELIA . . . . Portia Morrow

NORA . . . . Nellie Burt

MAGGIE . . . . Timothy Lynn Kearse

Directed by Bretaigne Windust.
Setting by Stewart Chaney

SYNOPSIS OF SCENES

The entire action takes place in the morning room of the Day house on Madison Avenue, New York City. The time is Spring, late in the 1880's.

ACT ONE

SCENE 1: Breakfast time. An early summer morning.

SCENE 2: Tea Time. The same day.

ACT TWO

SCENE 1: Sunday, right after church. A week later.

SCENE 2: Breakfast time. Two days later.

(During the Second Scene the curtain is lowered to denote a lapse of three hours.)

ACT THREE

SCENE 1: Mid-afternoon. A month later.

SCENE 2: Breakfast time. The next morning.

NOTES TO THE STAGE DIRECTOR

LIFE WITH FATHER is a play of innumerable detail. Therefore more stage directions have been included in the present text than is usual. Careful study of the stage business and the inclusion of as much as possible will be rewarding.

The living-room should have the clutter of the Victorian period. It will probably be impossible to find "console tables" called for to be placed against the back wall of the room on either side of the arch. In their place a secretary and a table, or even a sideboard, can be used. It is necessary, however, that each of these have a flat surface upon which a serving tray can be placed, and each must have a drawer. The sliding doors are tremendously effective, but again are not absolutely necessary. Perhaps heavy drapes which could be closed by a pull cord would be an effective substitute. Undoubtedly a substitute will have to be found for the china pug-dog used in Act 3. Any large china dog could be used, and the word "pug" changed to "china"; or some other Victorian objet d'art, which Vinnie could admire but Father dislike.

In a play of so many scenes it is important that the waits between scenes be as short as possible. The window on stage right was put in a separate flat hinged on it upstage side, so that this flat could be opened during changes. This opening can be used to bring on and take off a false table top already set for breakfast for the breakfast scenes in the second and third acts. This cuts down the length of the waits enormously. The period of the play is the late 1880's—the bustle period for women. In the last scene of the play, it is better if Vinnie wears white. She should look as if she were dressed to attend a wedding. The men at this time wore four-button coats with high lapels, usually single-breasted. The trousers should be without cuffs or creases. It is very simple to adapt modern clothes to give this effect. Clarence must have three suits. The first should be light in color so that some stitching in black thread down the side of his left-hand coat pocket can make it look as though it had been torn and obviously mended.

5

His second suit should be black. The third again should be light. The boys have sailor straw hats.

It is not necessary that Father, Vinnie and the children be redheaded. In the professional production, Father and Vinnie wore wigs and the children who were not redheaded had their hair dyed. Wigs do not look well on children. Hair can be painted red with ordinary water-color, although this does not work too well on dark hair. After drying, the hair should be combed gently and sprayed with brilliantine to give it sheen. But better no red hair than any attempt to achieve it that badly fails.

It is important, however, that the family be redheaded in temperament, vital and spirited. The household leads a life of shadow and sunshine. When Father is pleasant and hearty, the children are smiling and relaxed. When Father is angry, they are sober and watchful. Father, however, is hot-tempered, *not bad-tempered*. Vinnie is spirited and never a martyr. In the scenes where she stands up to Father with some spunk, she is at the same time never too sure of achieving victory. Father must never seem to be henpecked. In Vinnie's mind, as well as his own, he is the head of the house. They are both ingenuous and both without humor. Their differences never have the personal tinge of the ordinary family row. Once Father has laid down the law he expects the law never again to be broken, so that in each of his indignations there is incredulity and surprise. Vinnie is never scheming or calculating. She does try to postpone the meeting of household crises, but when they occur she uses nothing but her feminine instinct. She is feminine and Father is masculine and that is the entire basis of their conflict.

The Authors

LIFE WITH FATHER

ACT ONE

SCENE 1.

The morning room in the Day home at 420 Madison Avenue, New York City, which served both as a breakfast room and a living room for the family.

Upstage center is a wide archway, dividing the room from the hall. The archway can be closed by the use of sliding doors. It is usually open, however, and through it can be seen the stairs leading to the second floor, going up left, and below them the rail of the stair well leading to the basement. The front door, which we often hear slam, is to the right.

The room is furnished with the massive furniture of the period—which is the late 80's. The drapes and upholstery of most of the furniture are green.

The window, stage right, fronts on Madison Avenue. Down stage of the window is a large comfortable chair, upholstered in gold color, where Father generally sits to read his paper. Right of center is the table, which serves as a living room table, with its proper table cover and bowl of fruit, but at meal times it is expanded by extra leaves, and becomes a dining table. Left of center is a sofa.

In left wall, is a fine fireplace and mantle, over which is a very large mirror. There is a drape on the mantel and a clock, two vases, and two candelabras.

Against the back wall, upper left center and right center are large console or side tables which the maid uses as serving tables. There is a drawer in each of these.

A stand and large lamp are just left of the console table left center.

Right of Father's chair, down right, is a tabouret used as a smoking stand, on which there are a silver-topped glass jar of cigars, a match stand and ashtray, a small vase of flowers and two beautifully bound books.

Up right there is an upholstered bench, which is put below the table right when the room is not used as a dining room.

At the moment there is a large fancy table-cloth folded on this bench, which during the action of the first scene, is put on the table right center.

In the upper right and left corners of the room are stands upon which are large palms in handsome jardinieres.

Just above the right corner of the sofa is an occasional table, on which there is a lamp, two framed photographs and an imposing ornament.

To the left of the sofa is a small end table, which in Scene Two is moved to the front of the right end of the sofa and used as a tea table. At the moment, this table has on it a vase of flowers, three books, and an ornament.

Just below the fireplace is an ornament stand, properly dressed. And in front of it is a small armchair.

Just above the fireplace is a bell pull.

Above the window right is a small stand on which is a tall rubber plant in a handsome jardiniere.

There are a number of very fine paintings, beautifully framed, on the walls.

On the console table up left are a large vase of flowers and two smaller vases, also at the moment, there are four coffee cups and saucers, a tray, on which are four plates holding half an orange each and two small plates, cereal bowls of cereal, and a silver toast rack with toast.

On a console table up right there are a large vase of flowers, two smaller vases, and two small framed photographs. Also at the moment, there is a tray on which there are six napkins in silver rings.

The table right center is set for breakfast. Six plates, six knives and forks, six teaspoons, four fruit spoons, six pats of butter, four silver salt and pepper shakers, a silver sugar bowl and spoon, a silver cream pitcher. A bowl of fruit is in the center of the table.

8

A handsome five-light gas chandelier hangs from the ceil-
ing. Two handsome five-candle sconces are on the curved
walls, U.R. and U.L.
The clock on mantle says eight-thirty.
The Morning Times is on Father's armchair, down right.
As the curtain rises, ANNIE, *the new maid, is finishing set-*
ting the table. After an uncertain look at the result, she
crosses over to her tray on the side of console table up
left. Gets toast rack—takes it to the breakfast table—then
again returns to the console table U.L.C.
VINNIE *comes down the stairs and into the room. She has*
red hair.

VINNIE. Good morning, Annie.

ANNIE. Good morning, Ma'am.

VINNIE. How are you getting along?

ANNIE. All right, Ma'am, I hope.

VINNIE. Now don't be nervous, just because this is your first
day. Everything's going to be all right—but I do hope nothing goes wrong. (*She goes to back of table—then to* R. *of it.*)
Now, let's see, is the table all set? (*Surveys table and indicates
the cream pitcher and sugar bowl.* ANNIE *follows to above
table.*) The cream and the sugar go down at this end. (*Pointing to place near where Father's coffee cup will be placed.*)

ANNIE. (*Placing them where indicated.*) I thought in the
center, Ma'am; everyone could reach them easier.

VINNIE. Mr. Day sits here.

ANNIE. (*Getting tray of napkins from side table* R.C.) I didn't
know where to place the napkins, Ma'am.

VINNIE. You can tell which go where by the rings. (*She takes
one from tray*) This one belongs to Whitney—it has his ini-
tial on it—"W" (*She goes to below table and puts it at
R. downstage side. She picks up another.* ANNIE *follows her*)
This one with the little dog on it is Harlan's, of course. He's
the baby. (*She puts it at lower* L. *side of table. She picks up
another and crosses* L. *of table to above it*) (ANNIE *follows*)
This "J" is for John. (*Puts it at upper* L. *side of table. Then
picks up another*) The "C" is for Clarence—he sits here. (*Puts
it at upper* R. *side of table. Picks up another*). (ANNIE *is* L. *of*
VINNIE'S *chair*) This plain one is mine. (*Puts it at* L. *end of
table. Picking up last one*) And this one is Mr. Day's. It's just

9

like mine—except that it got bent—one morning. (*Puts it at* R. *end of table*) And that reminds me, Annie—always be sure Mr. Day's coffee is piping hot.

ANNIE. Ah, your man has coffee instead of tea of a morning?

VINNIE. (*At* R. *of table*) We all have coffee except the two youngest boys. They have their milk. And, Annie, always speak of my husband as Mr. Day.

ANNIE. I will that.

VINNIE. (*Correcting*) "Yes, ma'am, Annie."

ANNIE. Yes, ma'am.

VINNIE. And if Mr. Day should speak to you just say "Yes, sir." (*Crosses front of table to* C.) Don't be nervous—you'll get used to him. (ANNIE *puts tray on side table* U.R.C., *moving at same time that* VINNIE *does.* CLARENCE, *the eldest son, about seventeen, comes down the stairs and into the room. He is a manly, serious, goodlooking boy. Because he is starting in Yale next year he thinks he is grown up. He is redheaded. The* L. *pocket of his coat shows where it had been torn and mended*) (CLARENCE *take: "Yes, sir" as cue to start down stairs.*)

CLARENCE. (*At* C.L. *of* VINNIE) Good morning, Mother. (*He kisses her*)

VINNIE. Good morning, Clarence. (ANNIE *crosses to side table* U.L.C.)

CLARENCE. Did you sleep well, Mother?

VINNIE. Yes, dear.

CLARENCE. Good. (CLARENCE *crosses* D.R. *and picks up morning paper*)

VINNIE. (*To* ANNIE) We always start with fruit, except the two young boys who have porridge. (ANNIE *takes tray of four fruit and two cereals to table* R. *and places them from* R. *upper and* L. *upper corners of table*)

CLARENCE. (*Looking at newspaper*) Jimminy! Another wreck on the New Haven! That always disturbs the stock market. Father won't like that.

VINNIE. (*Coming* D.C.) I do wish that New Haven would stop having wrecks. If they knew how it upset your father—(*She indicates* CLARENCE's *torn and mended coat. Crosses to him*) Mercy! Clarence, what's happened to your coat?

CLARENCE. I tore it. Margaret mended it for me.

VINNIE. It looks terrible. Why don't you wear your blue suit?
CLARENCE. That looks worse than this one. You know, I burnt that hole in it.

VINNIE. You can't go around looking like that. (JOHN, *who is about fifteen, starts down stairs and into room.* JOHN *is red-headed*) I'll have to speak to your Father. Oh, dear! (VINNIE *crosses to* C.)

JOHN. (*Meeting* VINNIE *at* C.) Good morning, Mother. (*He kisses her*)

VINNIE. Good morning, John. (VINNIE *goes to* U.L. *corner of table*) (ANNIE *has finished at table, so crosses to* U.L.C. *to await orders*)

JOHN. (*Crossing* D.R.) Who won?

CLARENCE. I haven't looked yet.

JOHN. Let me see. (*He tries to take paper away from* CLARENCE)

CLARENCE. Be careful.

VINNIE. Boys,—don't wrinkle that paper before your Father's looked at it.

CLARENCE. (*To* JOHN) Yes! (VINNIE *turns to* ANNIE)

VINNIE. Annie, you'd better get things started. We want everything ready when Mr. Day comes down. (ANNIE *exits* C. *to* L. —*taking tray with her*) (*Suddenly remembering something*) Oh! (*Crossing* D.C.) Clarence, right after breakfast, I want you and John to move the small dresser from my room into yours.

CLARENCE. What for? Is somebody coming to visit us?

JOHN. (*Moves a few steps* L.) Who's coming?

VINNIE. (*Innocently*) I haven't said anyone was coming. (*Crosses* R. *to between boys with sudden thought*) And don't you say anything about it. I want it to be a surprise.

CLARENCE. (*Knowingly*) Oh! Father doesn't know yet!

VINNIE. No—and I'd better speak to him about a new suit for you before he finds out he's being surprised by visitors. (*Crosses* C. WHITNEY *comes running downstairs and rushes into room. He is about ten. Suiting his age, he is a lively active boy. He is red-headed*) (*He takes words "new suit for you" as cue to start down stairs*)

WHITNEY. (*Meets* VINNIE C.) Good morning, Mother. (*He kisses his mother quickly, then runs to* CLARENCE *and* JOHN)

11

VINNIE. Good morning, dear. (ANNIE *enters with two glasses of milk on a tray just as* WHITNEY *arrives at foot of stairs. She lets* WHITNEY *pass her. She places milk at* HARLAN's *and* WHITNEY's *places. She then crosses* U.L.C. *putting tray on side table there*) (VINNIE *goes to* U.L. *corner of table—a last look to be sure everything is in order*)

WHITNEY. Who won?

JOHN. The Giants, 7 to 3. Buck Ewing hit a home run. (HAR-LAN *comes sliding down bannister. He enters room. He runs to his mother and kisses her.* HARLAN *is a lovable, good-natured youngster of six. He is red-headed. He has a small removable finger bandage on first finger of* R. *hand*)

WHITNEY. Let me see.

HARLAN. Good morning, Mother.

VINNIE. (*Leading* HARLAN D.C.) Good morning, Darling. How's your finger?

HARLAN. It itches.

VINNIE. (*Kissing finger*) That's a sign it's getting better. Now don't scratch it. Sit down, boys. (*To* HARLAN) Get in your chair, darling. (BOYS *move to table and take their places.* CLARENCE *puts newspaper to* L. *of Father's place at table*) (JOHN *stands behind chair, ready to place* VINNIE's *chair when she sits.*) (WHITNEY *gets his oatmeal ready, with cream and sugar*) (VINNIE *goes up to* ANNIE) Now, Annie, watch Mr. Day; as soon as he has finished his fruit—(*There is a bellow from* FATHER *upstairs*)

FATHER'S VOICE. Vinnie! Vinnie! (*All eyes turn toward staircase*) (VINNIE *crosses to foot of stairs*)

VINNIE. What's the matter, Clare?

FATHER'S VOICE. Where's my necktie?

VINNIE. Which necktie?

FATHER'S VOICE. The one I gave you yesterday.

VINNIE. It isn't pressed yet. I forgot to give it to Margaret.

FATHER'S VOICE. I told you distinctly I wanted to wear that tie today.

VINNIE. You've got plenty of neckties. Put on another one right away, (*She starts toward her chair*) and come down to breakfast. (JOHN *moves to back of her chair*)

FATHER'S VOICE. Oh, damn!—Damnation! (*All react to* FA-THER's *damn*) (WHITNEY *starts to eat*) (JOHN *helps* VINNIE *into her chair*)

12

CLARENCE. Whitney!

VINNIE. Wait for your father, Whitney.

WHITNEY. But I'm in a hurry. John, can I borrow your baseball today? I'm going to pitch.

JOHN. (Sits) If I don't play myself.

WHITNEY. Look, if you need it, we're playing at the corner of Fifty-seventh Street.

VINNIE. Way up there!

WHITNEY. They're building a house on that vacant lot on Fiftieth.

VINNIE. (Putting napkin on her lap) My! My! My! Here we move to Forty-eighth Street just to get out of the city! (JOHN and CLARENCE take their napkins.)

WHITNEY. Can't I start breakfast, Mother? I promised to be there by eight o'clock.

VINNIE. After breakfast, Whitney, you have to study your catechism.

WHITNEY. Aw, Mother! Can't I do that this afternoon?

VINNIE. Whitney, you know you have to learn five questions every morning before you leave the house.

WHITNEY. Aw, Mother—

VINNIE. You weren't very sure of yourself when I heard you last evening.

WHITNEY. I know them now.

VINNIE. Let's see. (WHITNEY rises—stands R. of his chair, faces VINNIE) "What is your name?"

WHITNEY. Whitney Benjamin.

VINNIE. "Who gave you this name?"

WHITNEY. "My sponsors in baptism, wherein I was made a member of Christ, the child of God and an inheritor of the Kingdom of Heaven."—Mother, if I hadn't been baptized wouldn't I have a *name?*

VINNIE. Not in the sight of the church. "What did your sponsors then for you?"

WHITNEY. "They did promise and vow three things in my name—" (FATHER *makes his appearance on stairway.* FATHER *is about fifty, distinguished in appearance, with great charm and vitality, extremely well-dressed in a conservative way. He is red-headed*)

FATHER. (*Heartily interrupting* WHITNEY) Good morning,

boys. (*They rise and answer him*) (FATHER *enters the room*) Good morning, Vinnie.

VINNIE. Good morning, Clare.

FATHER. (*He goes to her and kisses her*) Did you have a good night?

VINNIE. Yes, thank you Clare.

FATHER. Good. (*Postman's whistle is blown twice then doorbell rings*) Sit down, boys. (FATHER *crosses to* R. *of table*)

VINNIE. That's the doorbell, Annie. (ANNIE *exits* C. *to* R.) Clare, that new suit looks very nice.

FATHER. Too damn tight! (*He sits*) What's the matter with those fellows over in London? I wrote them a year ago they were making my clothes too tight! (BOYS *dive into their breakfasts.* WHITNEY *passes cream and sugar to* HARLAN—*after he uses them,*—WHITNEY *replaces them near* FATHER)

VINNIE. You've put on a little weight, Clare.

FATHER. (*Putting his napkin on his knee*) I weigh just the same as I always have. (ANNIE *enters with mail on silver salver, starts to take it to* VINNIE) (*There are three letters— a blue envelope and letter addressed to* VINNIE—*a business letter from the "Gem Home Popper" addressed to* CLARENCE DAY, JR. *and an unimportant envelope of notepaper size addressed to* CLARENCE DAY, ESQ.) (*To* ANNIE) What's that? The mail? That goes to me. (ANNIE *gives mail to* FATHER *and exits with her tray, which she gets from* U.L.C. *She returns salver to* R.—*supposedly near front door—then crosses hall to* L.)

VINNIE. Clarence has just managed to tear the only decent suit of clothes he has.

FATHER. (*Looking through mail*) Here's one for you, Vinnie. John, hand that to your mother. (*He passes letter on to* VINNIE —*puts other two letters* R. *of his place, then starts on his breakfast*)

VINNIE. I'm sorry, Clare dear; but I'm afraid Clarence is going to have to have a new suit of clothes.

FATHER. Clarence has to learn not to be so hard on his clothes.

CLARENCE. Father, I thought—

FATHER. Clarence, when you start in Yale in the Fall, I'll set aside a thousand dollars just to outfit you,—but you'll get no new clothes this summer.

CLARENCE. Can't I have one of your old suits made over for

me?

FATHER. Every suit I own still has plenty of wear in it. I wear my clothes until they're worn out.

VINNIE. Well, if you want your clothes worn out, Clarence can wear them out much faster than you can.

CLARENCE. Yes, and Father, you don't get a chance to wear them out. (ANNIE *enters with tray on which is a pot of coffee and a platter of scrambled eggs and bacon. She puts tray down on side table* U.L.C. *then crosses to breakfast table, gets* VINNIE'S *and* JOHN'S *fruit-cup, puts them on tray on side table up* R.C.) Every time you get a new batch of clothes, Mother sends the old ones to the Missionary barrel. I guess I'm just as good as any old missionary. (JOHN *and* VINNIE *have finished their fruit*)

VINNIE. Clarence, before you compare yourself to a missionary, remember the sacrifices they make. (VINNIE *opens her letter and glances through it.* CLARENCE *has finished his fruit*)

FATHER. (*Has finished with his orange. Chuckling*) I don't know, Vinnie. I think my clothes would look better on Clarence than on some Hottentot. (*To* CLARENCE) Clarence, have that black suit of mine made over to fit you before your mother gets her hands on it. (VINNIE *takes piece of toast*) (ANNIE *takes* FATHER'S *fruit plate*)

CLARENCE. Thank you, Father. (*To* JOHN) Gee, one of Father's suits. Thank you, sir! (WHITNEY *is eating very rapidly*) (ANNIE *takes Clarence's fruit plate and places them on tray* U.R.C. *Then takes tray and fruit plates to side table* U.L.C. *She then pours two cups of coffee and prepares to serve bacon and eggs*) (VINNIE *is reading her letter*)

FATHER. Whitney, don't eat so fast.

WHITNEY. But, Father, I'm going to pitch today and I promised to get there early, but before I go I have to study my catechism.

FATHER. What do you bother with that for?

VINNIE. (*Shocked—looks up from letter suddenly*) If he doesn't know his catechism he can't be confirmed.

WHITNEY. (*Pleading to Mother*) But I'm going to pitch today.

FATHER. Vinnie, Whitney's going to pitch today and he can be confirmed any old time. (ANNIE *starts with platter of bacon and eggs to breakfast table*)

VINNIE. Clare, sometimes it seems to me that you don't care whether your children get to heaven or not.

FATHER. Oh, Whitney'll get to heaven all right. (*To* WHITNEY) I'll be there before you are, Whitney, I'll see that you get in. (ANNIE *has reached Father's side—she leans over so that the platter of bacon and eggs is very close to Father's plate.* FATHER *takes serving fork and spoon from platter*)

VINNIE. What makes you so sure they'll let you in?

FATHER. (*With good-humored gusto*) Well, if they don't, I'll certainly make a devil of a row. (ANNIE, *a very religious girl, is shocked, and draws back, raising platter*)

VINNIE. (*With shocked awe*) Clare, dear, I do hope you'll behave yourself when you get to heaven. (FATHER *turns to serve himself from platter, but* ANNIE *is holding it too high for him*)

FATHER. (*Storming*) Vinnie, how many times have I asked you not to engage a maid who doesn't even know how to serve properly?

VINNIE. (*Trying to quiet* FATHER) Clare, can't you see she's new and doing her best?

FATHER. How can I serve myself when she's holding that platter over my head?

VINNIE. Annie, why don't you hold it lower? (ANNIE *lowers platter. She is frightened.* VINNIE *reads her letter again*) (FATHER *serves himself but goes on talking*)

FATHER. Where'd she come from anyway? What became of the one we had yesterday? (ANNIE *goes to* CLARENCE *and* JOHN *and serves them. She begins to sniffle*) I don't see why you can't keep a maid.

VINNIE. (*Looks up from letter*) Oh, you don't!

FATHER. All I want is service. (FATHER *eats one bite of egg— then turns to* WHITNEY, *coming back to his genial tone*) Whitney, when we get to heaven we'll organize a baseball team of our own. (BOYS *laugh*)

VINNIE. (*Laughingly. Putting letter down*) It would be just like you to try to run things up there. (ANNIE *serves* VINNIE)

FATHER. Well, from all I've heard about heaven, it seems to be a very unbusinesslike place. They could probably use a good man like me. (FATHER, *after tasting bacon, swings his chair front and stamps on floor three times*) (*After* FATHER's *first stamp* ANNIE *goes* U.L.C. *She puts bacon and egg platter on tray with fruit)*

VINNIE. (*Anxiously*) What are you stamping for Margaret for? What's wrong? (ANNIE *has reached side table* U.L.C. *and is sniffling audibly.* FATHER *hears her but doesn't recognize the source)*

FATHER. (*Looking* R.) What's that damn noise? (ANNIE *sniffles again. The* FOUR BOYS *look at* ANNIE)

VINNIE. Shhh—it's Annie.

FATHER. Annie? Who's Annie?

VINNIE. The maid. (VINNIE *looks towards* ANNIE) (ANNIE, *seeing that she has attracted attention, cries loudly and hurries out into hall, taking tray of fruit and platter of bacon and eggs. After* ANNIE *exits* VINNIE *turns her head slowly toward* FATHER. *The heads of the four* BOYS *turn at same time.—All are looking at* FATHER) Clare, aren't you ashamed of yourself?

FATHER. (*Surprised*) What have I done now?

VINNIE. You made her cry—speaking to her the way you did.

FATHER. I never said a word to her—I was addressing myself to you. (*He eats again*)

VINNIE. I do wish you'd be careful. It's hard enough to keep a maid—and the uniforms just fit this one. (MARGARET, the *cook, a small Irishwoman of about fifty, comes into room from* L. *She is a little worried.*) (VINNIE *starts to read her letter again, while eating*)

MARGARET. What's wanting?

FATHER. Margaret, this bacon is good. (MARGARET *beams and gestures deprecatingly*) (ANNIE *enters, drying her eyes,—and goes* U.L.C.—*pours two more cups of coffee*) It's good. It's done just right!

MARGARET. Yes, sir! (*She smiles very pleased, and exits*) (*As* MARGARET *exits*—WHITNEY *passes rack of toast to* FATHER, *who takes a slice.* WHITNEY *takes one and passes it to* CLARENCE *who helps himself and passes it to* JOHN. *He serves himself and puts rack behind bowl of fruit on* C. *of table*)

VINNIE. Clare, this letter gives me a good idea. I've decided that next winter I won't give a series of dinners. (ANNIE *starts to table with two cups of coffee*)

FATHER. I should hope not.

VINNIE. I'll give a big musicale instead.

FATHER. You'll give a what?

17

VINNIE. A musicāle.

FATHER. (*Peremptorily*) Vinnie, I will not have my peaceful home turned into a Roman arena with a lot of hairy fiddlers prancing about.

VINNIE. I didn't say a word about hairy fiddlers. (ANNIE *places cup by* FATHER. *She is still afraid of him.* ANNIE *serves* CLARENCE, *then crosses* U.L. *and gets two other cups*) Mrs. Spiller has written me about this lovely young girl who will come for very little.

FATHER. What instrument does this inexpensive paragon play? (FATHER *uses cream and sugar*) (ANNIE *serves coffee to* JOHN *and* VINNIE, *then goes* U.L.C.) (*After* FATHER *has used cream and sugar* CLARENCE *uses them and passes them to* JOHN, *who uses them after* MOTHER *has served herself. Then they are returned to near* FATHER's *place*)

VINNIE. She doesn't play, Clare, she whistles.

FATHER. (*Astonished*) Whistles!!

VINNIE. She whistles sixteen different pieces. All for twenty-five dollars.

FATHER. I won't pay twenty-five dollars to any human peanut-stand! (*He tastes his coffee, grimaces, and stamps on floor three times*)

VINNIE. (*Using cream and sugar. Speaking after* FATHER's *third stamp*) Clare, I can arrange this so it won't cost you a penny. If I invite fifty people and charge them fifty cents apiece, there's the twenty-five dollars right there!

FATHER. You can't invite people to your own house and then charge them admission.

VINNIE. I can, if the money's for the missionary fund.

FATHER. Then where are you going to get the twenty-five dollars for her whistling?

VINNIE. (*Thinks it over for a second*) Now, Clare, let's cross that bridge when we come to it. (*Puts letter in envelope*)

FATHER. And if we do cross it—it will cost me twenty-five dollars—Vinnie, I'm going to be firm about this musicale—just as I had to be firm about keeping this house full of visiting relatives. Why can't we live here by ourselves in peace and comfort? (MARGARET *comes into room*)

MARGARET. (*Smiling*) What's wanting?

FATHER. (*Sternly*) Margaret, what is this? (*He holds his coffee cup out*)

MARGARET. (*Very concerned. Crosses to above table*) It's coffee, sir.

FATHER. It is not coffee! You couldn't possibly take water and coffee beans and arrive at that! (*Pointing at cup*) It's slops, that's what it is—slops! Take it away! Take it away, I tell you! (*Passes cup and saucer to L. hand and extends it to her*) (MARGARET *takes* FATHER's *cup and dashes out*) (ANNIE *hurriedly starts to take* VINNIE's *cup*)

VINNIE. Leave my coffee there, Annie! It's perfectly all right! (ANNIE *exits* C. *to* L. *after getting tray and coffee-pot from* U.L.C.)

FATHER. (*Angrily*) It is not. I swear I can't imagine how she concocts such an atrocity. I come down to this table every morning hungry—(*The heads of the four* BOYS *turn in unison towards* FATHER *as he speaks and towards* MOTHER *as she speaks.—All are at a tension until* FATHER *breaks it*)

VINNIE. Well, if you're hungry, Clare, why aren't you eating your breakfast?

FATHER. What?

VINNIE. If you're hungry, why aren't you eating your breakfast?

FATHER. (*Thrown out of bounds*) I am. (*He takes a mouthful of bacon, munches it happily and smiles, the tension is relieved and* EVERYONE *starts eating again.* FATHER's *eyes fall on* HARLAN) Harlan, how's that finger? (HARLAN *holds up finger.*) Come over here and let me see it. (HARLAN *goes to* FATHER's *side, taking off finger cap. Shows his finger*) (FATHER *puts on his glasses*) Well, that's healing nicely. Now don't pick that scab or it will leave a scar and we don't want scars on your fingers, do we? (*He chuckles*) (HARLAN *laughs*) I guess you'll know the next time that cats don't like to be hugged. It's all right to stroke them, but don't squeeze them. Now go back and finish your oatmeal. (WHITNEY *has finished his breakfast, so folds napkin and puts in ring*)

HARLAN. (*Crosses toward* C.) I don't like oatmeal.

FATHER. (*Kindly*) Go back and eat it. It's good for you.

HARLAN. (*Turns, faces* FATHER) But I don't like it.

FATHER. (*Quietly, but firmly*) I'll tell you what you like and what you don't like. You're not old enough to know about

19

such things.—You've no business not to like oatmeal. It's good.

HARLAN. (*Almost yelling*) I hate it.

FATHER. (*Sharply*) That's enough! We won't discuss it! Finish that oatmeal at once! (HARLAN *stares at* FATHER *defiantly for a second—then goes slowly to his chair, sits and starts to eat slowly*)

WHITNEY. (*Not speaking until* HARLAN *is seated*) I've finished my oatmeal. May I be excused?

FATHER. Yes, Whitney, you may go.

WHITNEY. Thank you, sir. (*He gets up quickly—pushes his chair under table and runs around* R. *of table*)

FATHER. (*Opening a letter, putting envelope to his* R.) Pitch a good game. (WHITNEY *has arrived in* L. *of arch, where he pauses just long enough to bow towards his parents—good manners in those days. He starts to exit* R. *hurriedly, but is stopped short by his* MOTHER'S *voice*)

VINNIE. Whitney!

WHITNEY. (*Quickly turning and starting to stairs*) I'm going upstairs, to study my catechism.

VINNIE. Oh, that's all right, dear. Run along. (WHITNEY *bolts up stairs*)

WHITNEY. (*Stopping on way up*) Harlan, you'd better hurry up and finish your oatmeal if you want to go with me. (*Exits*) (HARLAN *begins to eat faster*)

FATHER. (*Letter bewilders* FATHER) I don't know why I'm always getting damn fool letters like this!

VINNIE. What is it, Clare?

FATHER. "Dear Friend Day: We are assigning you the exclusive rights for Staten Island, to make a house-to-house canvas selling the Gem Home Popper for popcorn—."

CLARENCE. I think that's for me, Father.

FATHER. (*Loudly, annoyed*) Then why didn't they address it to Clarence Day, *Jr.*? (*He looks at envelope*) Oh, they did. (MARGARET *slips in hurriedly and puts a cup of coffee beside* FATHER, *and exits* C. *to* L.) I'm sorry, Clarence. I didn't mean to open your mail. (FATHER *hands letter and envelope to* CLARENCE. *Puts cream in his coffee, then picks up newspaper*) (CLARENCE *puts letter in his pocket*)

VINNIE. I wouldn't get mixed up in that, Clarence. People

like popcorn but they won't go all the way to Staten Island to buy it.

FATHER. (*Reading newspaper*) Chauncey Depew's having another birthday.

VINNIE. How nice. (CLARENCE *puts napkin in ring*)

FATHER. He's always having birthdays. Two or three a year. (*Exploding*) Damn! Another wreck on the New Haven!

VINNIE. Yes. Oh, that reminds me. Mrs. Bailey dropped in last evening.

FATHER. (*Looking at her*) Was she in the wreck? (JOHN *puts napkin in ring*)

VINNIE. No. She was born in New Haven. (FATHER *goes back to his paper*) Clarence, you're having tea Thursday afternoon with Edith Bailey. (*She puts napkin in ring*)

CLARENCE. Oh, Mother do I have to?

JOHN. (*Singing. The tune is the verse of "Ta-ra-ra boom-de-aye"*) "I like coffee, I like tea. I like the girls and the girls like me." (FATHER *drinks his fresh coffee*) (HARLAN *finishes oatmeal—folds and puts napkin in ring*)

CLARENCE. Well, the girls don't like me and I don't like them.

VINNIE. Edith Bailey's a very nice girl, isn't she, Clare?

FATHER. Edith Bailey? Don't like her. I don't blame Clarence. (FATHER *rises and goes to his chair by window and settles down to his newspaper and cigar, which he takes from cigar holder on smoking table.*) (*Others rise.* HARLAN *pushes his chair under table and exits upstairs.* ANNIE *enters with large tray, crosses behind* BOYS *to* R. *end of table and starts clearing that half*)

VINNIE. (*In a guarded tone*) Clarence, you and John go upstairs and—do what I asked you to.

CLARENCE. You said the small bureau, Mother?

VINNIE. Sh! Run along! (JOHN *and* CLARENCE *exit upstairs. We hear* HARLAN *yelling—"Whitney."* VINNIE *looks at* FATHER, *hoping he hadn't heard* CLARENCE) (MARGARET *enters* C. *from* L.)

MARGARET. If you please, ma'am, there's a package been delivered with a dollar due on it. Some kitchen knives.

VINNIE. Oh, yes, those knives from Lewis and Conger's. (VINNIE *puts letter in drawer of side table* U.R.C. *and gets her purse from drawer of side table, opening it, giving* MARGARET,

21

who is U.C., *a dollar*) Here, give this dollar to the man, Margaret. (MARGARET *exits* C. *to* L.)

FATHER. (*Getting cigar ready—a formal rite with him*) Make a memorandum of that, Vinnie. One dollar and whatever it was for.

VINNIE. (*Crossing* D.C., *looking into purse*) Clare, dear, I'm afraid I'm going to need some more money.

FATHER. What for?

VINNIE. You were complaining of the coffee this morning. Well, that nice French drip coffee-pot is broken—and you know how it got broken. (VINNIE *crosses to* FATHER) (ANNIE *has finished* R. *side of table and exits with loaded tray*)

FATHER. (*Putting cigar down. Taking out wallet*) Never mind that. As I remember, that coffee-pot cost five dollars and-something. I'll give you six dollars. (*He gives her a five-dollar bill and a one-dollar bill*) And when you get it, enter the exact amount in the ledger downstairs.

VINNIE. (*Puts money in purse*) Thank you, Clare.

FATHER. (*Putting wallet in pocket*) We can't go on month after month having the household accounts in such a mess.

VINNIE. (*Sit on arm of* FATHER's *chair*) No—and Clare dear, I've thought of a system that will make my bookkeeping perfect.

FATHER. I'm certainly relieved to hear that. What is it?

VINNIE. Well, Clare, you never make half the fuss over how much I've spent as you do over my not being able to remember what I've spent it for.

FATHER. Exactly. This house must be run on a business basis. That's why I insist on your keeping books.

VINNIE. That's the whole point, Clare. All we have to do is open charge accounts everywhere and the stores will do my bookkeeping for me.

FATHER. Wait a minute, Vinnie.

VINNIE. Then when the bills came in you'd know exactly where your money had gone.

FATHER. I certainly would.--Vinnie, I get enough bills as it is.

VINNIE. Yes, and those bills always help. They show you where I spent the money. Now, if we had charge accounts everywhere--

FATHER. Now, Vinnie,—I'm not so sure that—

VINNIE. (*Sweetly—putting her cheek on* FATHER's *head*) Clare, dear, don't you hate those arguments we have every month. I certainly do. Not to have those I should think would be worth something to you.

FATHER. (*Pleasantly*) Well, I'll open an account at Lewis and Conger's—and one at McCreery's to begin with—we'll see how it works out.

VINNIE. Thank you, Clare. (*Kisses his cheek, then starts up and puts purse in drawer of side table*) (*The smile fades from* FATHER's *face and he shakes his head doubtfully, then picks up his paper*) (VINNIE *to back of table*) Oh—the rector's coming to tea this afternoon.

FATHER. The rector? Well, I'm glad you warned me. I'll gɔ to the Club.—Don't expect me home until dinner time.

VINNIE. (*Crossing* D. *to back of* FATHER's *chair—a little to* R. *of it*) I wish you'd take a little more interest in the church, Clare.

FATHER. Getting me into heaven's your job, Vinnie. (*Lovingly to her*) If there's anything wrong with my ticket when I get there, you can fix it up. Everybody loves you so muc.i— I'm sure God must, too.

VINNIE. I'll do my best, Clare. It wouldn't be heaven without you.

FATHER. (*With gusto*) If you're there, Vinnie, I'll maɲage to get in some way—even if I have to climb the fence. (*Picks up his cigar again*)

JOHN. (*From upstairs*) Mother! Mother, we've moved it. Is there anything else? (VINNIE *crosses front of table towards* C.)

FATHER. (*About to light his cigar*) What's being moved?

VINNIE. Never mind, Clare. I'll come right up, John. (*She goes up a few steps and stops. She suddenly remembers that* CORA *may arrive very soon and she wants* FATHER *out of the house before* CORA *comes.—She glances towards clock on mantel*) (*Looks back at* FATHER, *who is lighting his cigar*) Oh, Clare, dear, it's eight-thirty. You don't want to be late at the office.

FATHER. Plenty of time. (VINNIE *looks nervously toward front door, then goes upstairs*) (FATHER *returns to his newspaper.* VINNIE *has barely disappeared when something in paper makes* FATHER *yell*) Oh, God! (VINNIE *comes tearing down-*

stairs and into c. *of room*)

VINNIE. What's the matter, Clare? What's wrong?

FATHER. Why did God make so many damn fools and Democrats?

VINNIE. (*Relieved*) Oh, politics. (*She turns and goes upstairs*)

FATHER. (*Shouting after her*) Yes, but it's taking the bread out of our mouths. (*Looks at paper again*)—It's robbery, that's what it is, highway robbery! Honest Hugh Grant! Honest! Bah! A fine Mayor you've turned out to be. (FATHER *looks* L. *as if the Mayor was in the room and he was talking directly to him*) If you can't run this city without raising our taxes every five minutes you'd better get out and let someone who can. Let me tell you, sir, the real estate owners of New York City are not going to tolerate these conditions any longer. Tell me this—are these increased taxes going into public improvements or are they going into graft—answer me that, honestly, if you can, Mr. Honest Hugh Grant! You can't! I thought so. Bah! (ANNIE *enters hearing* FATHER *talking, she goes into hall but seeing* VINNIE *coming downstairs she stops*) (ANNIE *must be sure not to look toward* L. *side of room*) (VINNIE *comes downstairs during the next speech, taking as cue the Word "Plundering" to start.*) If you don't stop your plundering of the pocketbooks of the good citizens of New York we're going to throw you and your boodle Board of Aldermen out of office. (*Reads paper again*)

VINNIE. (*In* c. *of arch*) Annie, why aren't you clearing the table?

ANNIE. Mr. Day's got a visitor.

FATHER. (*Looking up, still talking to Mayor*) I'm warning you for the last time.

VINNIE. Nonsense, Annie, he's just reading his paper. Clear the table. (VINNIE *goes off to* L.) (ANNIE *comes in timidly and starts to clear table at lower* L. *corner of it*)

FATHER. (*Speaks as* ANNIE *gets to table. Still lecturing Mayor*) We pay you a good round sum to watch after our interests and all we get is inefficiency! (ANNIE *looks around sheepishly and is surprised to find there is no one in room*) (FATHER *seems to be directing next speech to her*) I know you're a nincompoop and I strongly suspect you of being a scalawag. (AN-

24

NIE *stands there petrified*) (WHITNEY *comes running downstairs*) It's graft—that's what it is—Tammany graft—and if you're not getting it, somebody else is.

WHITNEY. (D.C.) Where's John? Do you know where John is? (*He looks from* FATHER *to* ANNIE, *who is frightened and hurries to get all the rest of dishes on tray*) (HARLAN *runs down stairs, starting on cue "Where's* JOHN")

FATHER. (*Looking right through* WHITNEY—*still talking to Mayor*) Dick Croker's running this town and you're just his catspaw. (VINNIE *comes in from downstairs*) (FATHER *goes right on talking*) (OTHERS *carry on their conversation right through his speech*)

HARLAN. (U.C.) Mother, where's John?

VINNIE. (U.C.) He's upstairs, dear. (*Then she crosses above sofa to mantel—just looking things over. Then crosses below sofa to* C. *for her next line*) (WHITNEY *runs up to stairway and up two steps*)

FATHER. And, as for you, Richard Croker—don't think that just because you're hiding behind these minions you've put in public office, you're going to escape your legal responsibilities.

WHITNEY. (*During* FATHER'S *speech, calling upstairs*) John, John, I'm going to take your baseball.

JOHN. (*Off-stage*) Don't you lose it! And don't forget to bring it back either!

WHITNEY. I won't. (HARLAN *and* WHITNEY *exit* R.)

VINNIE. (*Speaks on cue, "legal responsibilities," above* C.) Annie, you should have cleared the table long ago. (ANNIE *works fast from now on.*) (VINNIE *goes out in hall and upstairs as she is talking*)

FATHER. (*Rises*) Legal responsibilities—by gad, sir, I mean *criminal* responsibilities! (*Slams paper on chair. Crosses behind table up towards arch, taking off his glasses as he goes*)

VINNIE. (*Continuing—not waiting for any cue. Starting upstairs*) Now you watch Harlan, Whitney. Don't let him be anywhere the ball can hit him. Do what Whitney says, Harlan. And don't be late for lunch. (VINNIE *exits*)

WHITNEY. (*Off* R.) We won't. (*Door slams*)

FATHER. (*About* R.U. *corner of table*) (*Still talking to Mayor*) Don't forget what happened to William Marcy Tweed—

(*Crosses to arch* U.C.) (ANNIE *is again petrified*)—and if you put our taxes up once more, we'll put you in jail! (*He goes out of arch to* L. *A few seconds later he is seen passing arch toward outer door, wearing his hat and carrying his stick, puffing his cigar. Door is heard to slam loudly*) (ANNIE *has everything on tray, except fruit bowl. She seizes tray and runs out of arch to* L. *toward basement stairs. A second later, a scream and a tremendous crash is heard*) (JOHN *and* CLARENCE *come running downstairs and look over rail of stairs below*) (VINNIE *follows them almost immediately*)

VINNIE. (*On upper stairs*) What is it? What happened?

CLARENCE. The maid fell downstairs.

VINNIE. (*Coming down*) I don't wonder with your Father getting her so upset. (*Coming into room*) Why couldn't she have finished with the table before she fell downstairs? (CLARENCE *crosses behind* VINNIE, *toward window* R.)

JOHN. (*Coming to* VINNIE) I don't think she hurt herself.

VINNIE. Boys, will you finish the table! (*She starts* U.C.) (JOHN *crosses to table*) Don't leave the house, Clarence, until I talk to you. (*She exits to* L.)

JOHN. (*Taking dish of fruit from table, puts it on side table* U.R.C.) What do you suppose Mother wants to talk to you about?

CLARENCE. (*Pushing* FATHER's *chair away from table*) Oh, probably about Edith Bailey.

JOHN. (*To* L. *of table—pushes* VINNIE's *chair out of way*) What do you talk about when you have tea alone with a girl? (*During following speeches,* JOHN *and* CLARENCE *fold tablecloth and silencer as if it were one object—* JOHN *throws his end to* CLARENCE *to finish folding.*) (*Fold is really not the correct word, for they are very careless about it*) (JOHN *puts his chair up* R. *of arch—then opens drawer in side table.* CLARENCE *brings table-cloth up to him—he takes it and stuffs it in drawer as* CLARENCE *goes to* R. *of table.* JOHN *goes to* L. *of table and they pull table apart:* JOHN *takes one leaf—leans it against* L. *end of side table.* CLARENCE *has taken other leaf and goes up with it.* JOHN *takes it from him, puts it with other one. Then* JOHN *goes to* L. *of table and* CLARENCE *to* R. *of table—they push table together. Then* CLARENCE *gets fancy table-cloth from bench up* R. *and puts it on table,* JOHN *help-*

ing him. JOHN *places* VINNIE's *chair back near table—facing it front)*

CLARENCE. We don't talk about anything. I say "Isn't it a nice day?" And she says "Yes" and I say "I think it's a little warmer than yesterday," and she says, "Yes, I like warm weather, don't you?" And I say, "Yes" and then we wait for tea to come in. *(It is at this point that* JOHN *stuffs table-cloth in drawer as described above)* And then she says "How many lumps," and I say "Two, thank you," and she says "You must have a sweet tooth" and I can't say "Yes" and I can't say "No," so we just sit there and look at each other for a half an hour. Then I say, "Well, it's time I was going," and she says "Must you?" and I say "I've enjoyed seeing you very much" and she says "You must come again" and I say "I will" and get out.

JOHN. Some fellows like girls.

CLARENCE. I don't.

JOHN. And did you ever notice fellows, when they get sweet on a girl—the silly things a girl can make them do? And they don't even seem to know they are acting silly. *(He puts* CLARENCE's *chair* U.R.)

CLARENCE. Well, not for Yours Truly! (VINNIE *returns from downstairs* C. *from* L.) (CLARENCE *crosses to back of table)*

VINNIE. I declare I don't see how anyone could be so clumsy.

CLARENCE. Did she hurt herself?

VINNIE. No, she's not hurt—she's just hysterical, she doesn't even make sense. Your father may have raised his voice a little; and if she doesn't know how to hold a platter properly, she deserved it—but I know he didn't threaten to put her in jail. (VINNIE *crosses to back of table)* *(Then* JOHN *comes down* R. *of table—placing* FATHER's *chair to table, facing it front)* Oh, well! Clarence, I want you to move your things into the front room. You'll have to sleep with the other boys for a night or two.

CLARENCE. You haven't told us who's coming.

VINNIE. *(Happily)* Cousin Cora. Isn't that nice?

CLARENCE. It's not nice for me. I can't get any sleep in there with those children.

JOHN. Wait'll Father finds out she's here! There'll be a rumpus.

VINNIE. John, don't criticize your father. He's very hospitable —(*She smooths the table-cloth*) after he gets used to the idea. (*Doorbell rings*) (CLARENCE *moves up to side table* R.C.)

JOHN. (*Goes to lower side of window*) (VINNIE *goes to window, too*) (CLARENCE *gets bowl of fruit from side table—puts it* C. *of table*) Yes, it's Cousin Cora. Look, there's somebody with her.

VINNIE. (*Looking out*) She wrote me she was bringing a friend of hers. They're both going to stay here. (*A limping* ANNIE *passes through hall*) Finish with the room, boys. (*Crosses front of table to* U.C.)

CLARENCE. (*To* C.) Mother, do I have to sleep with the other boys and have tea with Edith Bailey all in the same week?

VINNIE. Yes, and you'd better take your Father's suit to the tailor's right away so it will be ready by Thursday. (VINNIE *goes down hall to* R. *to greet Cora and Mary*) (CLARENCE *goes quickly* D.L. *of table, gets* HARLAN's *chair and puts it* U.L. *of arch, then gets table leaves and exits* C. *to* L.) (JOHN *takes* WHITNEY's *chair to* U.L. *corner of room, then comes down to front of sofa.*—VINNIE (*offstage*) Cora dear—

CORA. Cousin Vinnie, I'm so glad to see you. This is Mary Skinner.

VINNIE. Ed Skinner's daughter? How do you do. Leave your bags right in the hall. Come right upstairs. (VINNIE *enters—going toward stairs.* CORA *follows her but seeing* JOHN, *she enters room and goes to him*) (MARY *enters as* VINNIE *goes down,* C.) (CORA *is an attractive woman of thirty*) (MARY *is a very pretty, wide-eyed girl of seventeen*)

CORA. Well, Clarence, it's so good to see you!

VINNIE. (*Comes down* R. *of* C.) Oh, no, that's John. (ANNIE *crosses* R. *to* L. *in hall*)

CORA. John! Why, how you've grown. You'll be a man before your mother. (*She laughs at her own wit then turns toward* C.) (MARY *has come down center*) John, this is Mary Skinner.

MARY. (*Crossing to* JOHN) How do you do. (JOHN *bows*)

CORA. This is Mary's first trip to New York. (CORA *crosses to* VINNIE) Oh, Vinnie, I have so much to tell you. We wrote you Aunt Carrie broke her hip. That was the night Robert Ingersoll lectured. Of course she couldn't get there; and it was a good thing for Mr. Ingersoll she didn't. (CLARENCE *enters*)

28

And Grandpa Ebbetts hasn't been at all well. (VINNIE *indicates Clarence's presence—*CORA *turns to him*)

CLARENCE. (D.C.) How do you do, Cousin Cora. I'm glad to see you.

CORA. (*At his* R.) This can't be Clarence.

VINNIE. Yes, it is.

CORA. (*Shakes his hand*) My goodness, every time I see you boys you've grown another foot. Let's see—you're going to St. Paul's now, aren't you?

CLARENCE. (*With pained dignity*) St. Paul's. I was through with St. Paul's long ago. (*Facing front; proudly*) I'm starting in Yale this Fall.

MARY (*Moves quickly to* CLARENCE. *Very interested*) Yale!

CORA. Oh, Mary, this is Clarence—Mary Skinner. (CLARENCE *nods.* MARY *smiles and says "How do you do"*) This is Mary's first trip to New York. (CLARENCE *smiles but abruptly turns and crosses back of table toward window. He doesn't like girls*) (VINNIE *crosses to* MARY *to cover up his seeming rudeness*) She was so excited when she saw a horse car.

VINNIE. We'll have to show Mary around. I'll tell you—I'll have Mr. Day take us all to Delmonico's to dinner tonight.

MARY. (*Delighted*) Delmonico's!

CORA. Oh, that's marvelous. Think of that, Mary—Delmonico's! And Cousin Clare's such a wonderful host.

VINNIE. (*Starting* C.) I know you girls want to freshen up. So come upstairs. (CORA *starts up*)

CORA. Is it straight up?

VINNIE. The same little room.

CORA. (*Going up stairs*) Oh, yes, I know the way. (*The above three lines are in the nature of an ad lib and must not be given any importance*) (VINNIE *is now at* R. *side in arch*) (MARY *follows up slowly until she is left of newel-post*)

VINNIE. Clarence, I'll let the girls use your room now and when they've finished you can move. And, bring up their bags. They're out in the hall. (VINNIE *starts upstairs, following* CORA *who has disappeared*) I've given you girls Clarence's room but he didn't know about it until this morning and he hasn't moved out yet. (VINNIE *has disappeared upstairs*)

CORA. (*Off-stage*) It's a shame to put him out. (MARY *follows more slowly and when she is up two steps she turns and leans*

29

towards CLARENCE) (CLARENCE *has gone into hall with his back toward* MARY)

CLARENCE. (*Speaking during last part of* VINNIE'S *speech*) John, get their old bags. (JOHN *runs—exits toward* C. *front door*) (CLARENCE *moves to* R. *of newel-post. Voices of* VINNIE *and* CORA *have trailed off into the upper reaches of the house*) (CLARENCE *turns to scowl in their direction and finds himself looking full into the face of Mary*)

MARY. Cora didn't tell me about you. I never met a Yale man before. (*She gives him a smile, then turns and goes quickly upstairs with an excited girlish whinney*) (CLARENCE *follows her up a step and stares after her a second, then turns toward audience with a look of "What happened to me just then?", and then a broad grin comes over his face*)

CURTAIN

ACT ONE

SCENE 2

The same day. Tea-time.
The clock says six-ten.
There is an upholstered bench front of table R.
The tea service is on VINNIE'S R. VINNIE *and the* RECTOR *are having tea. The* REV. DR. LLOYD *is a plump, bustling man, very good-hearted and pleasant,* VINNIE *and* DR. LLOYD *have one strong point in common: their devotion to the church and its rituals.* VINNIE'S *devotion comes from her natural piety;* DR. LLOYD'S *is a little more professional.*

AT RISE: *At rise* DR. LLOYD *is seated* D.L. *in arm-chair—with cup of tea.*

VINNIE *is seated on* R. *end of sofa.*

WHITNEY *is standing near* DR. LLOYD, *stiffly erect in the manner of a boy reciting.*

HARLAN *is seated on sofa, beside his mother, leaning against her and watching* WHITNEY'S *performance.*

30

WHITNEY. (*Reciting*) ". . . to worship Him; to give Him thanks; to put my whole trust in Him, to call upon Him . . ." (*He hesitates*)

VINNIE. (*Prompting*) "To honor—"

WHITNEY. "To honor His Holy Name and His Word—and to serve Him truly all the days of my life." (*He bows to* DR. LLOYD, *then turns towards his mother, hoping that is the end*)

DR. LLOYD. "What is thy duty toward thy neighbor?" (WHITNEY *knows this is a tough one, shakes his head and goes "whew." Then he pulls himself together and makes a brave start*)

WHITNEY. "My duty toward my neighbor is to love him as myself, and to do to all men as I would they should do unto me; to love, honor and succor my father and mother; to honor and obey . . .

VINNIE. "—Civil authorities!"

WHITNEY. (*Very quickly*) "Civil authorities.—*To*—to—" (*When Whitney says first "to" he is smiling because he is confident that he knows the rest.—Suddenly the smile fades from his face as he realizes he doesn't remember; the second "to" is said very uncertainly*)

VINNIE. (*To* DR. LLOYD) He really knows it.

WHITNEY. I know most of the others.

DR. LLOYD. He's done very well for so young a boy. I'm sure if he applies himself between now and Sunday, I could hear him again—with the others.

VINNIE. There, Whitney, you'll have to study very hard if you want Dr. Lloyd to send your name in to Bishop Potter next Sunday.

WHITNEY. Yes, Mother.

VINNIE. I must confess to you, Dr. Lloyd, it's really my fault. Instead of hearing Whitney say his catechism this morning, I let him play baseball.

WHITNEY. (*Excitedly to* DR. LLOYD) We won, too; thirty-five to twenty-seven.

DR. LLOYD. That's splendid, my child. I'm glad your side won. But winning over your catechism is a richer and fuller victory.

WHITNEY. (*To his mother, almost pleadingly*) May I go now?

VINNIE. Yes, darling. Thank Dr. Lloyd for hearing you and

31

run along.

WHITNEY. Thank you, Dr. Lloyd.

DR. LLOYD. Not at all, my little man. (WHITNEY *bows to* DR. LLOYD, *then starts out quickly but sees the cake on tea-tray, so he slyly but quickly turns back—grabs a piece and runs out, hesitating at arch to give a very quick bow. He exits* R. *and we hear front door slam*) (*During above business,* VINNIE *and* DR. LLOYD *are drinking their tea*)

VINNIE. Little Harlan is very apt at learning things by heart.

HARLAN. (*Rises—to* DR. LLOYD) I can spell Constantinople. Want to hear me?

DR. LLOYD. Constantinople?

HARLAN. Yes sir, C-o-ennaconny—annaconny—sissaconny—tan-tan-tee-and anople and a pople and a Constantinople! (HARLAN *laughs*)

DR. LLOYD. (*Laughingly*) Very well done, my child.

VINNIE. (*Putting her tea-cup on tray and handing* HARLAN *a a cake from tea-tray*) That's nice, darling. This is what you get for saying it so well.

HARLAN. (*Quickly taking cake*) Oh! (*Then to* DR. LLOYD) Want me to say it again for you?

VINNIE. No, darling. One cake is enough. You run along and play with Whitney.

HARLAN. (*To* DR. LLOYD) I can spell huckleberry-pie.

VINNIE. Run along, dear. (HARLAN *goes out, skipping in rhythm to his recitation.* C. *to* R.)

HARLAN. H-a-huckle—b-a-buckle—h-a-huckle—high. H-a-huckle—b-a-buckle huckleberry-pie! (*We hear door slam as he joins* WHITNEY)

DR. LLOYD. (*Rises. Crosses to* VINNIE—*amused*) You and Mr. Day must be very proud of your children.

VINNIE. (*Beaming*) Yes, we are.

DR. LLOYD. (*He sits on sofa beside her, hands his cup and saucer to her*) Thank you.—I was hoping I'd find Mr. Day at home this afternoon.

VINNIE. (*Evasively*) Well, he's usually home from the office by this time.

DR. LLOYD. Perhaps he's gone for a gallop in the park—it's such a fine day. He's very fond of horseback riding, I believe.

VINNIE. Oh, yes.

DR. LLOYD. Tell me—has Mr. Day ever been thrown from a horse?

VINNIE. Oh no—no horse would throw Mr. Day.

DR. LLOYD. I've wondered. I thought he might have had an accident. I notice he never kneels in church.

VINNIE. Oh, that's no accident. But I don't want you to think Mr. Day doesn't pray. He does. Why, sometimes, you can hear him pray all over the house. But he never kneels.

DR. LLOYD. Never kneels! Dear me! (*He rises, crosses to his chair* D.L. *and sits*) I was hoping to have the opportunity to tell you and Mr. Day about our plans for the New Edifice.

VINNIE. I'm so glad we're going to have a new church.

DR. LLOYD. I'm happy to announce that we're now ready to proceed. The only thing left to do is raise the money.

VINNIE. No one should hesitate about contributing to that! (*Front door slams*)

DR. LLOYD. Perhaps that's Mr. Day now.

VINNIE. (*She is sure that it isn't*) Oh, no, I hardly think so. (FATHER *appears in arch from* R. *He sees Rector—stops suddenly*)

FATHER. Oh, damn. I forgot.

VINNIE. (*Very flustered—Rises, crosses* U.C. *rear* L. *of arch*) Clare dear. Dr. Lloyd's here for tea.

FATHER. (*Trying to smile*) I'll be right in. (*He disappears almost dejectedly to* L. VINNIE *goes to bell-pull, pulls it—then to back of sofa*)

VINNIE. I'll order some fresh tea.

DR. LLOYD. Now we can tell Mr. Day about our plans for the New Edifice.

VINNIE. (*Knowing her man*) Yes—after he's had his tea. (*Crosses back of sofa—up to arch.* FATHER *enters room and walks front of sofa to down* L., *to greet the Rector*) (DR. LLOYD *rises*) (VINNIE *follows* FATHER *to front of sofa*)

FATHER. (*Speaking as he enters*) How are you, Dr. Lloyd? (CLARENCE *enters downstairs*)

CLARENCE. Oh, it was Father.

DR. LLOYD. Very well, thank you. (THEY *shake hands*)

CLARENCE. (*To* VINNIE) They're not back yet?

VINNIE. (*Waving her hand to him to go*) No! Clarence, no! (CLARENCE *turns, disappointed, and goes back upstairs*)

DR. LLOYD. It's a great pleasure to have a visit with you, Mr. Day. Except for a fleeting glimpse on the Sabbath, I don't see much of you. (FATHER *indicates to* DR. LLOYD *to sit down*) (DR. LLOYD *sits* D.L.) (DELIA, *the new maid, appears in arch and comes down* C. *taking word cue "glimpse" to start*)

DELIA. (C.) Yes, Ma'am.

VINNIE. (*Sits* R. *end of sofa*) Some fresh tea for Mr. Day. (DELIA *takes teapot from table and exits* C. *to* L.) (FATHER *sits* L. *end of sofa, not noticing* DELIA) (VINNIE *hurriedly starts conversation*) Well, Clare, did you have a busy day at the office?

FATHER. Damn busy.

VINNIE. (*In a whisper, touching his arm with her* R. *hand*) Clare!

FATHER. (*Smiling, to* DR. LLOYD) Very busy day. Tired out.

VINNIE. I've ordered some fresh tea. (*To* DR. LLOYD) Poor Clare, he must work very hard. He always comes home tired. Although, how a man can get tired just sitting at his desk all day, I don't know. (FATHER *gives her a quiet astonished look*) I suppose Wall Street is just as much a mystery to you as it is to me, Dr. Lloyd.

DR. LLOYD. No, no, it's all very clear to me. My mind often goes to the business man. The picture I'm most fond of is when I envisage him at the close of the day's work. There he sits—this hard-headed man of affairs, surrounded by the ledgers that he has been studying closely and harshly for hours. (FATHER, *bored, looks away*) I see him pausing in his toil— and by chance he raises his eyes and looks out of the window at the light in God's sky and it comes over him that money and ledgers are dross. (FATHER *stares at* DR. LLOYD *with some amazement*) He realizes that all those figures of profit and loss are without importance or consequence—(VINNIE *looks toward arch—hoping that* DELIA *will interrupt*) vanity and dust. And I see this troubled man bow his head and with streaming eyes resolve to devote his life to far higher things.

FATHER. (*Staring at him amazed*) Well, I'll be damned! (DR. LLOYD, *wrapt up in his little sermon, doesn't hear* FATHER. DELIA *enters with fresh tea for* FATHER. *She puts pot on table and stops to arrange cups, etc. She is* R. *of tea-table*)

VINNIE. (*Pouring tea*) Here's your tea, Clare. (FATHER *notices new maid*)

FATHER. Who's this?

VINNIE. (*Quietly—handing tea, on saucer of which is a piece of cake—to* FATHER) The new maid.

FATHER. Where's the one we had this morning? (DELIA *picks up cake plate—extends it towards* FATHER *and* VINNIE)

VINNIE. Never mind, Clare.

FATHER. The one we had this morning was prettier. (DELIA *puts plate down—tosses her head and hurriedly exits,* C. *to* L.) (FATHER *attacks cake with relish*) Vinnie, these cakes are good.

DR. LLOYD. Delicious!

VINNIE. (*Again trying to start conversation*) Dr. Lloyd wants to tell us about the plans for the New Edifice.

FATHER. The new what?

VINNIE. The new church—Clare, you know that we were planning to build a new church?

DR. LLOYD. Of course, we're going to have to raise a large sum of money.

FATHER. (*Alive to the danger*) Well, personally, I'm against the church hop-skipping and jumping all over town. And it so happens that during the last year I've suffered heavy losses in the market—damned heavy losses—

VINNIE. (*Again in whisper, touches his arm with her* R. *hand*) Clare!

FATHER. So any contribution I make will have to be a small one.

VINNIE. But, Clare, for so worthy a cause!

FATHER. —And if your Finance Committee thinks it's too small they can blame the rascals that are running the New Haven Railroad.

DR. LLOYD. The amount each one is to subscribe has already been decided.

FATHER. (*Bristling*) Who decided it?

DR. LLOYD. After considerable thought, we've found a formula which we believe is fair and equitable. It apportions the burden lightly on those least able to carry it, and justly on those whose shoulders we know are stronger. We've voted that our supporting members shall each contribute a sum equal to the cost of his pew.

FATHER. (*Indignantly*) I paid five thousand dollars for my pew.

VINNIE. Yes, Clare. That makes our contribution five thousand dollars.

FATHER. That's robbery! Do you know what that pew is worth today? Three thousand dollars. (*To* DR. LLOYD) That's what the last one sold for. I've taken a dead loss of two thousand dollars on that pew already. (*Starts to lift cup but next thought stops him*) Old Frank Baggs sold me his pew when the market was at the peak. He knew when to get out. (*Stares at* DR. LLOYD *a second, then turns to* VINNIE) And I'm warning you now, Vinnie, if the market ever goes up, I'm going to unload that pew. (*He drinks his tea*)

VINNIE. Clarence Day, how can you speak of the Temple of the Lord as though it was something to be bought and sold on Wall Street!

FATHER. Vinnie, this is a matter of dollars and cents and that's something you don't know anything about!

VINNIE. You talking of religion in terms of dollars and cents seems to me pretty close to blasphemy.

DR. LLOYD. (*Soothingly*) Now, Mrs. Day, your husband is a business man and he has a practical approach toward this problem. We've had to be practical about it, too—we have all the facts and figures.

FATHER. Oh! Well. (*Giving tea-cup to* VINNIE) What's the new piece of property going to cost you?

DR. LLOYD. I think the figure I've heard mentioned is $85,000 —or was it $185,000?

FATHER. What's the property worth where we are now?

DR. LLOYD. Well, there's quite a difference of opinion about that.

FATHER. (*Becoming a little annoyed at* DR. LLOYD'S *vagueness*) How much do you have to raise to build the new church?

DR. LLOYD. Now, I've seen those figures—let me see—I know it depends somewhat upon the amount of the mortgage.

FATHER. Mortgage? What are the terms of the amortization?

DR. LLOYD. Amortization? That's not a word I'm familiar with.

FATHER. It all seems very vague and unsound to me. (*Doorbell rings*) I certainly wouldn't let any customer of mine invest on what I've heard.

DR. LLOYD. We've given it a great deal of thought. I don't see

36

how you can call it vague. (DELIA *crosses hall* L. *to* R.)

FATHER. (*After a moment, speaking rather kindly*) Dr. Lloyd, you preach that some day we'll all have to answer to God.

DR. LLOYD. We shall indeed!

FATHER. (*Speaking firmly*) Well, I hope God doesn't ask you any questions with figures in them. (*We hear front door close. CORA'S voice is heard in hall, thanking DELIA*) (VINNIE *goes to arch just in time to meet* CORA *and* MARY *as they enter*) (CORA *carries a corset box and* MARY *has two small bonnet boxes. MARY puts bonnet boxes on side table* U.R. *and goes around* R. *of table—to front of bench* R.C.) (FATHER *rises*)

CORA. Oh, Vinnie, what a day. We've been to every shop in town and—

FATHER. (*Crossing* C.) Cora!

CORA. Cousin Clare! (*Crosses* D.R. *of* C.) (DR. LLOYD *rises as* LADIES *enter*)

FATHER. (*Cordially*) What are you doing in New York? (DELIA *enters, carrying about six packages of different sizes—*SHE *puts them with bonnet boxes on side table* U.R.C.*—then waits there arranging flowers, etc.*)

CORA. We're just passing through on our way to Springfield.

FATHER. We? (CLARENCE *comes downstairs into room. Crosses above table to* D.R.)

VINNIE. (*Crosses* D.L. *of* C.—*between* FATHER *and* DR. LLOYD) Oh, Dr. Lloyd, this is my favorite cousin, Miss Cartwright, and her friend, Mary Skinner. (*Mutual how-do-you-do's*)

DR. LLOYD. This seems to be a family reunion. I'll just run along.

FATHER. (*Promptly*) Goodbye, Dr. Lloyd.

DR. LLOYD. Goodbye, Miss Cartwright, goodbye, Miss—er— (CLARENCE *has been standing to one side with his eyes on* MARY)

VINNIE. Clarence, you haven't said how-do-you-do to Dr. Lloyd.

CLARENCE. (*So intent on* MARY, *he doesn't realize what he is saying*) Goodbye, Dr. Lloyd.

VINNIE. I'll go to the door with you. (FATHER *bows to* DR. LLOYD) (DR. LLOYD *and* VINNIE *go out talking,* U.C. *to* R.) (DELIA *crosses down to tea-table—ready for orders*)

FATHER. Cora, this is certainly a pleasant surprise. Have some tea with us. (*To* DELIA) Bring some fresh tea—and some more of those cakes.

CORA. Oh, we've had tea! (FATHER *indicates to* DELIA *to leave —SHE picks up tea table—puts it behind sofa—then takes tray and exits* C. *to* L.) We were so tired shopping, we had tea downtown.

MARY. (*A great treat to a country girl*) —At the Fifth Avenue Hotel.

FATHER. At the Fifth Avenue Hotel, eh? (*Crosses to* MARY R.C.) Who'd you say this pretty little girl is?

CORA. She's Ed Skinner's daughter. (FATHER *shakes her hand. She curtsies*) Well, Mary, at last you've met Mr. Day. I've told Mary so much about you, Cousin Clare, that she's just been dying to meet you.

FATHER. (*Indicating bench to* MARY *and sofa to* CORA, *who crosses to it.* FATHER *is* C.) Well, sit down. Sit down (MARY *sits on bench* R.C.) Even if you have had tea you can stop and visit for awhile. (*To* MARY) As a matter of fact, why don't you both stay to dinner? (VINNIE *enters just in time to hear this, and cuts in quickly*)

VINNIE. (*Crossing down between* FATHER *and* CORA) That's all arranged, Clare. Cora and Mary are going to have dinner with us.

FATHER. That's fine. That's fine.

CORA. (*Sitting on sofa*) Cousin Clare, I don't know how to thank you and Vinnie for your hospitality.

MARY. Yes, Mr. Day.

FATHER. (*To* MARY) Well, you'll have to take pot luck.

CORA. No, I mean—

VINNIE. (*Close to* FATHER—*quickly interrupting*) Clare, dear, did you know the girls are going to visit Aunt Judith in Springfield for a whole month?

FATHER. A whole month. (*Crossing* VINNIE—*towards sofa*) How long are you going to be in New York, Cora?

CORA. All week.

FATHER. Splendid. We'll hope to see something of you.

CORA. Why—we are—

VINNIE. (*Crossing to* CORA. *Quickly*) Did you find anything you wanted in the shops?

CORA. Just everything. (FATHER *moves to* R. *of* C.)

38

VINNIE. (*Trying to get* CORA *out of room*) I want to see what you got.

CORA. I just can't wait to show you. (*Rises. Crosses* VINNIE— *stops at* L. *of* FATHER. *Coyly to* FATHER, *indicating package in her hand, half hiding it*) Oh! I'm afraid some of the packages can't be opened in front of Cousin Clare.

FATHER. Shall I leave the room? (FATHER *laughs first, then* THEY *all join in. All but* VINNIE)

CORA. (*On* FATHER'S L.) Clarence, do you mind taking the packages up to our room, or should I say your room? (CLAR-ENCE *goes up to side table* U.R.C. *To* FATHER) Wasn't it nice of Clarence to give up his room to us for a whole week? (MARY *rises, crosses* U.C.) (FATHER *has a sudden drop in temperature*)

VINNIE. (*More anxious to get* CORA *out*) Come on, Cora, I just can't wait to see what's in those packages. (CORA, MARY *and* VINNIE *start upstairs.* CORA *first—*MARY *second.* CLARENCE *is gathering up packages*)

FATHER. (*Crosses to* D.R. *Ominously*) Vinnie, I wish to speak to you before you go upstairs.

VINNIE. I'll be down in just a minute, Clare. (*She starts upstairs*)

FATHER. (*Firmly*) I wish to speak to you now! (CORA *and* MARY *have disappeared upstairs*)

VINNIE. (*Stops short on stairs*) I'll be up in just a minute, Cora. (*We hear a faint "all right" from upstairs.* VINNIE *moves slowly toward* FATHER. *As* VINNIE *comes in room*)

FATHER. (*His voice is low but incredulous*) Are those two women encamped in this house?

VINNIE. Now, Clare!

FATHER. (*Louder*) Answer me, Vinnie!

VINNIE. (*Very hurriedly—starting towards* U.C.) Just a minute—

FATHER. (*Much louder*) Answer me!

VINNIE. Control yourself, Clare. (VINNIE, *scenting coming storm, hurries to sliding doors.* CLARENCE *has reached hall with his packages and he too has recognized the danger signal, and as* VINNIE *closes one door,* HE *closes other, closing himself out into the hall. As door closes* VINNIE *turns and smiles shyly at* FATHER) (*Persuasively. Coming down towards him*) Now, Clare, you know you've always been fond of Cora.

FATHER. What has that to do with her planking herself down in my house and bringing hordes of strangers with her?

VINNIE. (*Sweetly reproachful*) How can you call that sweet little girl a horde of strangers?

FATHER. Why don't they go to a hotel? New York is full of hotels built for the express purpose of housing such nuisances.

VINNIE. Clare! Two girls alone in a hotel. Who knows what might happen to them?

FATHER. (*Crosses to c. Exploding*) All right. Then put 'em on the next train. (*Turns to* VINNIE) If they want to roam—the damned gypsies (*Crosses to L. of c.*)—lend 'em a hand. Keep 'em roaming! (*Goes L. of c.—then to up c.*)

VINNIE. (*Following him to his L.*) What have we got a home for if we can't show a little hospitality?

FATHER. I didn't buy this home to show hospitality—I bought it for my own comfort!

VINNIE. (*Pleadingly*) How much are they going to interfere with your comfort living in that little room of Clarence's?

FATHER. The trouble is, damn it, they don't live there! They live in the bathroom. (*Crosses to back of table R.C.*) (VINNIE *moves to R. of sofa*) Every time I want to take my bath it's full of giggling females washing their hair. From the time they take, you'd think it was the Seven Sutherland Sisters. (*Crosses to R. of table*) Get them out of here. Send 'em to a hotel. I'll pay the bill, gladly, but get them out of here. (CLARENCE *looks in through sliding doors*)

CLARENCE. Father, I'm afraid they can hear you upstairs.

FATHER. (*Very matter-of-fact*) Then keep these doors closed! (CLARENCE *starts to close them*)

VINNIE. (*At L. of c. With spirit, but quietly*) Clarence!—you open those doors—open them all the way. (CLARENCE *does so and stands L. of arch*) (VINNIE, *lowering her voice, crossing to L. of table R.C. but maintaining her spirit*) Now, Clare, you behave yourself! They're here and they're going to stay here.

FATHER. (*With great dignity*) That's enough, Vinnie! I want no more of this argument. (*With a nod of decision he goes to his arm-chair below window, muttering*) Damnation! (*He sits*)

CLARENCE. Mother, Cousin Cora's waiting for you.

40

FATHER. What I don't understand is why this swarm of lo-custs always descends on us without any warning. (VINNIE *is convinced of her victory, so starts upstairs*) Damn! Dam-nation! (*He looks toward stairs*) Damn! ! ! (VINNIE *disappears up stairs*) (*Helplessly*) Vinnie. (*He remembers that he loves her and chuckles*) Dear Vinnie. (*He remembers that he is angry with her*) Damn!

CLARENCE. (*Crosses to* R. *front of table*) Father, can't I go along with the rest of you to Delmonico's tonight?

FATHER. What's that? Delmonico's?

CLARENCE. You're taking Mother, Cora and Mary to Delmoni-co's for dinner.

FATHER. (*Explodes*) Oh, God! (*Rises and crosses to* L.C.) (*At this sound from* FATHER, VINNIE *comes flying downstairs again.* CLARENCE *quickly gets out of way by going up* R. *of table*) I won't have it.—I won't have it. (*He crosses* L.)

VINNIE. (*On the way down*) Clarence! The doors! (VINNIE *and* CLARENCE *rush and close sliding doors again.* CLARENCE *stays* U.R. *of arch*)

FATHER. I won't stand it, by God! I won't stand it! I won't submit myself . . . (*After doors are closed* VINNIE *goes down and faces* FATHER, *who is* D.L.)

VINNIE. (*Very simply and sweetly*) What's the matter now, dear?

FATHER. (*Quietly intense*) Do I understand that I am not to be allowed to have dinner in my own home?

VINNIE. (*Lovingly—crossing to him*) It'll do us both good to get out of this house. You need a little change. It'll make you feel better.

FATHER. (*Still quiet*) I have a home to have dinner in.—Any time I can't have dinner at home, this house is for sale!

VINNIE. (*Quietly stating a fact*) Well, you can't have dinner here tonight, because it isn't ordered.

FATHER. (*Exploding. Crossing to* U.C.) I'm ready to sell this place this very minute if I can't live here in peace. (*Turns facing* VINNIE) Then we can all go and sit under a palm tree and live on bread-fruit and pickles.

VINNIE. (*Crossing to* R. *of sofa*) But, Clare, Cora and Mary want to see something of New York.

FATHER. Oh, that's it! (*Crossing up* C. *to doors*) Well, that's

41

no affair of mine. (*Faces* VINNIE) I am not a guide to China-town and the Bowery. (*He throws open sliding doors, first* L. *one, then* R. *one*) (MARY *comes tripping down stairs as* HE *opens first door. She is wearing a charming party dress.* FATHER *is at* R. *of arch*)

MARY. (*In* C. *of arch*) Oh, Mr. Day, I just love your house. I could live here forever. (FATHER *draws himself up and continues on upstairs.* MARY *looks after* FATHER, *then comes into room, a little wide-eyed*) Cora's waiting for you, Mrs. Day.

VINNIE. Oh, yes, I'll run right up. (*She goes upstairs. There is a slight pause—*MARY *moves towards* D.L.C. *after a glance over her shoulder at* CLARENCE)

CLARENCE. I'm glad you like our house.

MARY. Oh, yes, I like it very much. (*Stops front of sofa and touches green sofa cushion*) I like green.

CLARENCE. (*Crossing to her*) I like green myself.

MARY. (*Looks up at his red hair rather shyly*) Red's my favorite color.

CLARENCE. (*Abashed, he can't look at her*) It's an interesting thing about colors. Red's a nice color in a house, too, but outside, too much red would be bad. I mean, for instance, if all the trees and the grass were red—(*Now he has control of himself and turns to her*)—outside, green is the best color.

MARY. (*Impressed*) That's right! I've never thought of it that way—but when you do think of it, it's quite a thought.—I'll bet you'll make your mark at Yale.

CLARENCE. (*Pleased, but modest*) Oh!

MARY. My mother wants *me* to go to college. Do you believe in girls going to college?

CLARENCE. I guess it's all right if they want to waste that much time—before they get married, I mean. (*Door slams and* JOHN *comes in, bringing the Youth's Companion. He stops* C. *of arch long enough to throw his hat off* L., *as if he threw it on hat rack.* HE *makes a whistling sound as he throws it*)

JOHN. Oh, hello! (*They say "Hello" to him*) Look! A new Youth's Companion! (JOHN *hurriedly crosses front of table to arm-chair,* D.R.)

CLARENCE. (*To* MARY—*from a mature height*) John enjoys the Youth's Companion. (JOHN *sits right down in* FATHER's *arm-*

chair D.R. *and starts to read.* CLARENCE *is worried by this*) John! (JOHN *looks at him non-plussed*) (CLARENCE *gestures for him to get up*) (JOHN *remembers his manners and stands*) (*Formally to* MARY) Won't you sit down?

MARY. Oh, thank you. (*She sits*) (JOHN *sits down again quickly and dives back in Youth's Companion*) (CLARENCE *turns as if to tell* JOHN *he may sit now, but* JOHN *has beaten him to it.* CLARENCE *sits beside* MARY)

CLARENCE. As I was saying—I think it's all right for a girl to go to college if she goes to a girls' college.

MARY. Well, mother wants me to go to Ohio Wesleyan because it's Methodist. (*Then almost as a confession*) You see, we're Methodists.

CLARENCE. Oh, that's too bad. (*Quickly correcting himself*) I don't mean it's too bad that you're a Methodist. Anybody's got a right to be anything they want. But what I mean is— (*Unhappily*) We're Episcopalians.

MARY. Yes, I know. I've known ever since I saw your minister—and his collar—(*She looks pretty sad for a moment, and then her face brightens*) Oh, I just remembered—my father was an Episcopalian. He was baptized an Episcopalian. He was an Episcopalian right up to the time he married my mother. (*Almost bitterly*) She was the Methodist.

CLARENCE. (*Enthusiastically*) I'll bet your father's a nice man.

MARY. (*Brightening*) Yes, he is. He owns the livery stable.

CLARENCE. He does? Then you must like horses. (FATHER *starts down stairs*)

MARY. Oh, I love horses!

CLARENCE. (*Very manly*) They're my favorite animal. Father and I both think there's nothing like a horse! (FATHER *comes into room.* CHILDREN *all stand*)

MARY. (*Crossing toward him*) Oh, Mr. Day, I'm having such a lovely time here.

FATHER. Clarence is keeping you entertained, eh?

MARY. Oh, yes, sir. (*She crosses quickly back to* CLARENCE, *then faces* FATHER) We've been talking about everything—colors—and horses—and religion—

FATHER. Hm-m. (*He turns to* JOHN) Has the evening *Sun* come yet?

JOHN. No, sir.

43

FATHER. (*Crosses to back of table*) What are you reading?
(CLARENCE *invites* MARY *to go* U.L. CLARENCE *shows her the stereoscope and pictures which are on console table* U.L.C.)
(*We hear front door slam*)

JOHN. The *Youth's Companion*, sir. (WHITNEY *and* HARLAN *run in from hall*) (HARLAN *goes to lower* L. *corner of table* R.C. WHITNEY *carries a box of tiddle-de-winks*)

WHITNEY. (*To* L.U. *corner of table*) Look what we've got!

FATHER. What is it?

WHITNEY. (*Opening box*) Tiddle-de-winks. We put our money together and bought it.

FATHER. That's a nice game. Do you know how to play it?

WHITNEY. (*Taking cup and tiddle-de-winks out of box*) I've played it lots of times.

HARLAN. Show me how to play it.

FATHER. (*Takes cup and tiddle-de-winks from* WHITNEY'S *hand*) Here, I'll show you, Harlan. (FATHER *arranges the things.* WHITNEY *goes below table* D.R. *corner—leans on table.* HARLAN L. *of table*)

MARY. Are you going out to dinner with us tonight?

CLARENCE. (*Looking at* FATHER) I don't know yet—but it's beginning to look as though I might.

FATHER. It's easy, Harlan. You press down like this and snap the little fellow into the glass. Now watch me—(*He snaps it and it goes off table, toward* C. FATHER *is as surprised as the boys*) The table isn't quite large enough. You boys better play on the floor. (FATHER *crosses towards* D.L. *of* C.) (FATHER *points to tiddle-de-wink on the floor—*HARLAN *gets it*) (CLARENCE *puts stereoscope away*) (MARY *crosses to below* L. *of sofa—*CLARENCE *joins her there*)

WHITNEY. (*To floor front of table.* THEY *take box of tiddle-de-winks with them and start to play*) Come on, Harlan, I'll take the reds and you take the yellows. (JOHN *crosses back of table as if to leave room*)

FATHER. John.

JOHN. (*Stops* R. *of arch*) Yes, sir.

FATHER. Have you practiced your piano today?

JOHN. I was going to practice this evening.

FATHER. Better do it now. (VINNIE *and* CORA *start down stairs, quickly, talking as they come*)

CORA. Don't say anything to Cousin Clare.

VINNIE. I will, too.

CORA. Please, Cousin Vinnie. (*Above three lines are in the nature of an ad lib and must not interfere with* FATHER's *line*)

FATHER. (*To* MARY) Music is a delight in the home. (CORA *and* VINNIE *enter room*) (JOHN *waits for* VINNIE *and* CORA *to enter—then exits to* L.) (CORA *stays up a little*)

VINNIE. (D.C.) Clare, what do you think Cora has just told me? (*She brings* CORA *down to* FATHER) (CORA *is between* FATHER *and* VINNIE) She and Clyde are going to be married this Fall.

FATHER. So, you finally landed him, eh? (EVERYBODY *laughs*) (VINNIE *crosses and sits on bench*) Well, Cora, he's a very lucky man. Being married, Cora, is the only way to live. (*From next room we hear* JOHN *playing "The Happy Farmer."*)

CORA. (*At* C.) Well, if we can be half as happy as you and Cousin Vinnie. (*Sits* L. *of table*) (FATHER *listens a moment to* JOHN's *piano-playing—then goes to sofa* L.C.)

VINNIE. (*On bench*) Boys, shouldn't you be playing that on the table?

WHITNEY. The table isn't big enough. Father told us to play on the floor.

VINNIE. My soul and body, look at your hands! (THEY *do so*) And your supper almost ready. Go wash your hands right away and come back and show Mother they're clean. (BOYS *pick up tiddle-de-winks saying "Yes, Mother," and depart quickly*)

FATHER. (*Sitting down on sofa, indicating to* MARY *to join him, which* SHE *does*) Vinnie, this young lady looks about the same age you were when I came out to Pleasantville to rescue you.

VINNIE. Rescue me! You came out there to talk me into marrying you.

FATHER. It worked out just the same.—I saved you from spending the rest of your life in that one-horse town.

VINNIE. (*Rises*) Cora, the other day I came across a tin-type taken of Clare in Pleasantville. I want to show it to you. You'll see who needed rescuing. (SHE *goes up* R. *of table to console table,* R. *of arch and starts to rummage around in drawer*)

FATHER. There isn't time for that, Vinnie—hadn't we all better be getting dressed—if we're going to Delmonico's for dinner? (*He includes* CLARENCE *and* MARY *with a look—looks at his watch*) (MARY *and* CLARENCE *exchange pleased looks*) It's after six now!

CORA. (*Rises*) Gracious! I'll have to start. (FATHER *and* MARY *rise*) If I'm going to dine in public with a prominent citizen like you, Cousin Clare—I'll have to look my best. (SHE *crosses to arch*)

MARY. I'm changed already.

CORA. Yes, I know, Mary, but I'm afraid I'll have to ask you to come along and hook me up. (CORA *goes to foot of stairs*)

MARY. (*Crossing—front of* FATHER *to* U.C.) Of course. (FATHER *moves a little to* R., *ready to bow to* LADIES *as they leave room*)

CORA. Won't take a minute, then you can come right back. (*Going up a step or two*) (MARY *turns and looks back at* FATHER) (CLARENCE *has gone up behind sofa to* L. *of arch*)

MARY. (*A little afraid to ask, but it is so important to her*) Mr. Day,—were you always an Episcopalian?

FATHER. What?

MARY. (C.) Were you always an Episcopalian?

FATHER. I've always gone to the Episcopal church, yes.

MARY. But you weren't baptized a Methodist or anything, were you? You were baptized an Episcopalian?

FATHER. Come to think of it, I don't believe I was ever baptized at all. (MARY, *a little shocked, joins* CORA *on stairs*)

VINNIE. Clare, that's not very funny, joking about a subject like that.

FATHER. I'm not joking—I remember now—(*To* MARY) I never was baptized. (*Above table* R.)

VINNIE. Clare, that's ridiculous, everyone's baptized.

FATHER. (*Sits on sofa*) Well, I'm not.

VINNIE. Why, no one would keep a little baby from being baptized.

FATHER. You know Father and Mother—Free Thinkers, both of them—believed their children should decide those things for themselves.

VINNIE. But, Clare—

FATHER. I remember when I was ten or twelve years old, Mother said I ought to give some thought to it. (JOHN *finishes playing piano*) I suppose I thought about it, but I never got around to having it done to me. (VINNIE *walks slowly down toward* FATHER, *staring at him in horror*) (FATHER *is quite happily curling his moustache*) (*There is a decided pause*)

VINNIE. (*Quietly*) Clare, do you know what you're saying?

FATHER. I'm saying I've never been baptized.

VINNIE. (*Excitedly*) Then something has to be done about it right away!

FATHER. Now, Vinnie; don't get excited over nothing.

VINNIE. Nothing? I've never heard of anyone who wasn't baptized. Even the savages in darkest Africa—

FATHER. (*Matter of factly*) It's all right for savages—and children. But if an oversight was made in my case it's too late to correct it now.

VINNIE. Clare, why haven't you ever told me?

FATHER. (*Getting a little annoyed*) What difference does it make?

VINNIE. But you're not a Christian, if you're not baptized.

FATHER. (*Rises—exploding*) Why, confound it, of course I'm a Christian. A damn good Christian, too. (FATHER R.) (CLARENCE *rushes to sliding doors and quickly closes them—shutting himself,* MARY *and* CORA *out*) A lot better Christian than those psalm-singing donkeys in church. (*He crosses back to* VINNIE)

VINNIE. You can't be if you won't be baptized.

FATHER. I won't be baptized and I will be a Christian. I'll be a Christian in my own way.

VINNIE. Clare, don't you want to meet us all in heaven?

FATHER. Of course, and I'm going to.

VINNIE. You can't, unless you're baptized.

FATHER. (*Crosses to* D.R.) That's a lot of folderol.

VINNIE. (*Following him to front of bench*) Clarence Day,— don't you blaspheme like that. You're coming to church with me before you go to the office in the morning and be baptized then and there.

FATHER. Vinnie, don't be ridiculous! If you think I'm going to stand there and have some minister splash water on me at my age,—you're mistaken.

VINNIE. But, Clare—

FATHER. (*Firmly*) That's enough, Vinnie. (*He thinks for a second*) I'm hungry. (*Crosses up* c.) I'm dressing for dinner. (FATHER *goes to doors and opens them.* WHITNEY *and* HARLAN *are there, leaning over as if listening at keyhole.* THEY *straighten up quickly*) (FATHER'S *attention is on door he had opened, so he passes to* R. *of boys and starts up stairs before he notices them. He hesitates only a moment, then stalks upstairs*) (*The* TWO BOYS *look after* FATHER *and then come down into room, staring at their mother*)

WHITNEY (*Awed—remembering what Mother had told him at breakfast—not speaking until they are* D.C.) Mother, if Father hasn't been baptized he hasn't any name. In the sight of the church he hasn't any name.

VINNIE. That's right! (SHE *sinks on bench. To herself*) Maybe we're not even married! (*This awful thought takes possession of* VINNIE. HER *eyes turn slowly toward children, and she suddenly realizes their doubtful status.* HER *hand goes to her mouth to cover a quick gasp of horror as* CURTAIN FALLS)

CURTAIN

ACT TWO

Scene 1

The same.

The following Sunday. After church. A stool is L. *of* FATHER'S *armchair* D.R. *The tea table is again at* L. *of sofa, with its ornaments on it. The clock says twelve-thirty. The stage is empty as curtain rises.*

VINNIE *comes into arch from street door, dressed in her Sunday best, carrying her prayer book, and a cold indignation. She looks over her shoulder—toward front door —then comes down to front of chair* L. *of table—turns her back on audience, and watches as*

FATHER *passes across hall, in his Sunday cutaway, gloves and cane, and wearing his silk hat.*

As FATHER *disappears,* VINNIE *drops her prayer book rather heavily on table, and starts to take off her gloves —still facing toward arch.*

HARLAN, CORA *and* WHITNEY *come into room.*

JOHN *follows them on, and goes off* L., *to hang up his hat.*

HARLAN. (*Pulling* CORA *to back of sofa and indicating tiddle-de-winks box which is on mantel*) Cousin Cora, will you play a game of tiddle-de-winks with me before you go?

CORA. I'm going to be busy packing until it's time to leave.

WHITNEY. We can't play games on Sunday.

CORA. (*As* JOHN *enters from* L. *and starts upstairs*) John, where are Clarence and Mary?

JOHN. They dropped behind—way behind! (JOHN *goes upstairs*) (CORA *crosses to window*) (WHITNEY *takes* HARLAN'S *hat from him and starts toward arch*)

VINNIE. Whitney, don't hang up your hat. I want you to go to Sherry's for the ice-cream for dinner. (HARLAN *goes to* WHITNEY) Tell Mr. Sherry strawberry—if he has it. And take Harlan with you.

WHITNEY. Yes, Mother. (WHITNEY *hands* HARLAN *his hat; then* THEY *bow to their mother—then put on their hats, turn and*

49

exit C. *to* R., HARLAN *following* WHITNEY. *We hear door slam*)
CORA. (*Crosses to* R. *of table*) Oh, Vinnie, I hate to leave!
We've had such a lovely week.
VINNIE. (*Taking off her hat—puts it on table. Sits* L. *of table*)
Cora, what must you think of Clare, making such a scene on
the way out of church?
CORA. Cousin Clare probably thinks that you put the Rector
up to preaching that sermon.
VINNIE. Well—I had to go to Dr. Lloyd to find out whether
we were really married. The sermon on baptism was his own
idea. If Clare just hadn't shouted so—now the whole congregation knows he's never been baptized. But he's going to be,
Cora—you mark my words—he's going to be. I just couldn't
go to Heaven without Clare. Why, I get lonesome for him
when I go to Ohio. (FATHER *enters from* C. *from* L., *his watch
in his hand*)
FATHER. (*At* C.) Vinnie, I went to the dining-room and the
table isn't even set for dinner yet.
VINNIE. We're having dinner late today.
FATHER. Why can't I have my meals on time?
VINNIE. The girls' train leaves at half-past one. Their cab's
coming for them at one o'clock.
FATHER. (*Crosses back of sofa—to mantel*) Cab? The horse
cars go right past our door.
VINNIE. They have those heavy bags.
FATHER. (*Sets clock by his watch*) Clarence and John could
have gone along to carry their bags. Cabs are just a waste of
money. Why didn't we have an early dinner? (FATHER *crosses
to front of sofa* L.)
VINNIE. There wasn't time for an early dinner and church,
too.
FATHER. As far as I'm concerned this would have been a very
good day to miss church.
VINNIE. (*Rises—spiritedly*) I wish we had.
FATHER. (*Flaring*) I'll bet you put him up to preaching that
sermon. (CORA *moves* U.R. *to get out of the seeming quarrel*)
VINNIE. (*Crossing to* L.C.) I've never been so mortified in all
my life. You stamping out of church, roaring your head off
at the top of your voice.
FATHER. (*Crossing* R.C.) That Lloyd needn't preach at me as

50

though I were some damn criminal. I wanted him to know it, (*Turns to* c.) and as far as I'm concerned, the whole congregation can know it, too.

VINNIE. They certainly know it now.

FATHER. That suits me.

VINNIE. (*Crossing to him,* c. *Pleading*) Clare, you don't seem to understand what the church is for.

FATHER. Vinnie, if there is one place the church should leave alone, it's a man's soul. (*Crosses to* L.C.)

VINNIE. (*Moves toward him*) Clare, dear, don't you believe what it says in the Bible?

FATHER. (*Smilingly*) A man has to use his common sense about the Bible, Vinnie, if he has any! For instance, you'd be in a pretty fix if I gave all my money to the poor.

VINNIE. (*After a moment's thought*) Oh,—that's just silly. (*Crosses to* L. *of table*)

FATHER. Speaking of money—where are this month's household bills?

VINNIE. (*Turning quickly*) Now, Clare,—it isn't fair to go over the household accounts while you're hungry.

FATHER. Where are those bills, Vinnie?

VINNIE. They're downstairs on your desk. (FATHER *exits* c. *to* L.) Of all times! (VINNIE *sits* L. *end of bench* R.C.) (*To* CORA) It's awfully hard on a woman to love a man like Clare so much.

CORA. (*Moves down and sits on bench beside her*) Yes, men can be aggravating. Clyde gets me so provoked. We kept company for six years, but the minute he proposed, that is, from the moment I said "Yes," he began to take me for granted.

VINNIE. You have to expect that, Cora. I don't believe Clare has come right out and told me he loves me since we've been married. Of course I know he does, because I keep reminding him of it.—You have to keep reminding them, Cora. (*Door slams*)

CORA. There's Mary and Clarence. (*There is a moment's pause, then the* TWO WOMEN *look towards hall—then at each other with a knowing sort of smile.* CORA *rises, goes up to* L. *side of arch—peeks out—then faces front and says innocently*) Is that you, Mary?

MARY. (*Dashes in—very flustered*) Yes. (CLARENCE *crosses arch.*

with great dignity, wearing black suit and a straw hat. He exits L. to hang up hat)

CORA. Well! We have to change our clothes and finish our packing. (CORA *goes upstairs*) (MARY *follows her*) (CLARENCE *enters*) (VINNIE *takes up hat, etc.—starts up* C. *as if to follow* MARY *upstairs*)

MARY. *(On first step. To* CLARENCE*)* It won't take me long.

CLARENCE. Can I help you pack?

VINNIE. *(Shocked)* Clarence! (MARY *runs upstairs*) (CLARENCE *turns into living-room, somewhat abashed, and goes* D.L. *of* C.) (VINNIE *puts her hat and gloves back on table, looks at* CLARENCE*)* Clarence, why didn't you kneel in church today?

CLARENCE. (D.L. *of* C.) What, Mother?

VINNIE. Why didn't you kneel in church today?

CLARENCE. I just couldn't.

VINNIE. *(Crosses to him)* Has it anything to do with Mary? I know she's a Methodist.

CLARENCE. Oh, no, Mother. Methodists kneel. Mary told me. They don't get up and down so much, but they stay down longer.

VINNIE. If it's because your Father doesn't kneel—you must remember he wasn't brought up to kneel in church. But you were—you always have—and, Clarence, you want to, don't you?

CLARENCE. Oh, yes. I wanted to today. I started to—you saw me start—but I just couldn't.

VINNIE. Is that suit of your Father's too tight for you?

CLARENCE. *(Crosses* D.R.C.) No, it's not too tight. It fits fine. *(Stops, turns to* VINNIE*)* But it is the suit.—Very peculiar things have happened to me since I started to wear it. I haven't been myself since I put it on.

VINNIE. *(Crossing to* CLARENCE*)* What do you mean, Clarence? What do you mean? (CLARENCE *pauses, then blurts out his problem*)

CLARENCE. Mother, I can't make these clothes do anything Father wouldn't do.

VINNIE. That's nonsense—(CLARENCE *moves to* R.)—and not to kneel in church is a sacrilege.

CLARENCE. *(Coming back to* VINNIE*)* But making Father's trousers kneel is more of a sacrilege.

52

VINNIE. Clarence!

CLARENCE. No! Remember the first night I wore this? It was at Dora Wakefield's party for Mary. Do you know what happened? We were playing Musical Chairs and Dora Wakefield sat down suddenly right in my lap. I jumped up so fast she almost got hurt.

VINNIE. But it was all perfectly innocent.

CLARENCE. It wasn't that Dora was sitting on my lap—she was sitting on Father's trousers. Mother, I've got to have a suit of my own. (*Moves* R. *a little*)

VINNIE. My soul and body! Well, Clarence, you have a talk with your Father. (VINNIE *follows him to* R.C.) (MARY *hurries downstairs*) I'm sure if you approach him the right way—you know—tactfully—he'll see—(MARY *comes into room*)

MARY. Oh—excuse me.

VINNIE. (*Turning to* MARY) Gracious, have you finished your packing already?

MARY. Practically. I never put my comb and brush in until I'm ready to close my bag.

VINNIE. (*She pats her son's arm, then crosses around* L. *of table to back of it—to get hat, etc.*) I must see Margaret about your box lunch for the train. (MARY *moves to back of chair* L. *of table, looking starry-eyed at* CLARENCE) I'll leave you two together. (VINNIE *crosses up to arch*) Remember—it's Sunday. (*Exits to* L.) (*After a short embarrassed pause,* MARY *moves* D.C.)

CLARENCE. I was hoping we could have a few minutes together before you left.

MARY. (*Not to admit her eagerness. Crosses to* L. *front of sofa*) Cora had so much to do I wanted to get out of her way.

CLARENCE. (*Following her*) Didn't you want to see *me?*

MARY. (*Self-consciously*) I did want to tell you how much I have enjoyed our—friendship. (*"Friendship" almost sounds like "love"*)

CLARENCE. You're going to write me when you get to Springfield, aren't you?

MARY. Of course, if you write first.

CLARENCE. But you'll have something to write about—your trip and Aunt Judith—and how things are in Springfield. You write to me as soon as you get there.

MARY. (*Rather coyly. Sits*) Maybe I'll be too busy. Maybe I won't have time.

CLARENCE. (*Sounding like his Father*) You find the time! Let's not have any nonsense about that! (MARY *at first is very surprised at his tone—then she smiles happily—impressed by his manliness.—He sits*) You'll write me first—and you'll do it right away, the first day!

MARY. (*Egging him on*) How do you know I'll take orders from you?

CLARENCE. I'll show you. (*Takes quick glance toward the hall—then holds out his L. hand*) Give me your hand!

MARY. Why should I?

CLARENCE. (*Very much like* FATHER) Give me your hand, confound it!

MARY. (*Innocently*) What do you want with my hand? (*She lifts her hand so it's near his, but doesn't give it to him*)

CLARENCE. (*He takes her hand, sharply*) I just—(*Holding her hand, he melts*) wanted it.

CLARENCE. (*Their hands, clasped together, rest on* CLARENCE'S *knee and they relax happily. After a moment* MARY *looks away*) What are you thinking about?

MARY. I was just—thinking.

CLARENCE. About what?

MARY. Well, when we were talking about writing each other, I was hoping you would write me first because that would mean that you liked me.

CLARENCE. What's writing first got to do with my liking you?

MARY. (*Turns to him*) Oh, you do like me?

CLARENCE. Of course I do. I like you better than any girl I ever met.

MARY. (*Rather triumphantly*) But you don't like me well enough to write first?

CLARENCE. I don't see how one thing's got anything to do with the other.

MARY. (*A little flustered*) But a girl can't write first because—she's a girl.

CLARENCE. (*Thinks that over for a second*) That doesn't make sense. If a girl has something to write about and a fellow hasn't, there's no reason why she shouldn't write first.

MARY. (*Taking a different tack—being a little hurt*) You know,

54

the first few days I was here you'd do anything for me, and then you changed. You used to be a lot of fun—and then all of a sudden you turned into an old sober-sides.

CLARENCE. When did I?

MARY. The first time I noticed it was when we walked home from Dora Wakefield's party. My, you were on your dignity. You've been that way ever since. You even dress like an old sober-sides. (CLARENCE's *face changes as* FATHER'S *pants rise to haunt him. Then he notices that their clasped hands are resting on these very pants, and he lifts them off, and lets go of her hand. Agony obviously is setting in*) (MARY *sees the expression on his face*) What's the matter?

CLARENCE. (*So tense his voice is husky*) I just happened to remember something.

MARY. What? (CLARENCE *doesn't answer*) Oh, I know. This is the last time we'll be together. (MARY *puts hand on his shoulder*)

CLARENCE. (*Afraid to have her even touch* FATHER'S *coat*) Mary, please.

MARY. But, Clarence—we'll see each other in a month. And we'll be writing each other, too.—I hope we will. (*She gets up, facing him, leaving her handkerchief on sofa*) Oh, Clarence, please write me first because it will show me how much you like me. Please! I'll show you how much I like you! (*She crosses in front of him, throws herself in his lap and buries her head on his* L. *shoulder*) (CLARENCE *stiffens*)

CLARENCE. (*Hoarsely—not looking at* MARY) Get up! Get up! (SHE *pulls back her head and looks at him, then springs from his lap with a loud cry and runs to* D.R.C., *covering her face and sobbing loudly* CLARENCE *gets up and goes to her*) Don't do that, Mary! Please don't do that!

MARY. (*Crying*) Now you'll think I'm just a bold and forward girl.

CLARENCE. Oh, no!

MARY. Yes, you will!—you'll think I'm bold!

CLARENCE. Oh, no—it's not that.

MARY. (*Half turning to him*) Was it because it's Sunday?

CLARENCE. No, it would be the same any day—(*He is about to explain, but* MARY *flares*)

MARY. (*Faces him*) Oh, it's just because you didn't want me

55

sitting on your lap?

CLARENCE. It was nice of you to do it—

MARY. It was nice of me! So you told me to get up! You just couldn't bear to have me sit there. Well, you needn't write me first. You needn't write me any letters at all because I'll tear them up without opening them! (*She turns her back on him, still crying*) (FATHER *enters arch from* L., *a sheaf of bills in his account book under his arm; also a pencil*) I guess I know now you don't like me. (*She breaks and starts to run toward stairs, around* R. *of table*) I never want to see you again. I—I—(*At sight of* FATHER *she stops, only to let out a louder cry, then continues on upstairs, unable to control her sobs*) (CLARENCE *who has been standing in unhappy indecision, turns to follow her around* R. *of table, but stops short,* R.U. *corner of table, at sight of* FATHER, *who is standing in arch, looking at him with some amazement*) (FATHER *looks toward the vanished* MARY, *and then back to* CLARENCE)

FATHER. Clarence, that young girl is crying—she's in tears. What's the meaning of this?

CLARENCE. I'm sorry, Father, it's all my fault.

FATHER. Nonsense! What's that girl trying to do to you?

CLARENCE. What? No, she wasn't—it was—I—how long have you been here?

FATHER. (*Crossing to back of table. Dismissing it*) Well, whatever the quarrel was about, Clarence, I'm glad you held your own. Where's your mother?

CLARENCE. (*Desperately*) I have to have a new suit of clothes —you've got to give me the money for it. (FATHER'S *account-book reaches the table with a sharp bang as he stares at* CLARENCE *in astonishment*)

FATHER. Young man, do you realize you're addressing your father? (CLARENCE *wilts miserably*)

CLARENCE. I'm sorry, Father—I apologize—(*He crosses* D.R. *and sinks on stool just* L. *of* FATHER'S *armchair*)—but you don't know how important this is to me.

FATHER. A suit of clothes is so—? Now why should a—? (*Something dawns on* FATHER, *he looks up in direction in which* MARY *has disappeared, then looks back at* CLARENCE. *Crosses* L. *of table to* R.C.) Clarence, has your need for a suit of clothes anything to do with that young lady?

CLARENCE. Yes, Father.

FATHER. Why, Clarence! (FATHER *suddenly realizes that women have come into* CLARENCE'S *emotional life, and there comes a yearning to protect this inexperienced and defenseless member of his own sex*) This comes as quite a shock to me.

CLARENCE. What does, Father?

FATHER. You're being so grown-up. Still, I might have known that if you're going to college this fall—yes, you're at an age when you'll be meeting girls—Clarence, there are things about women that I think you ought to know. (*He goes up and closes doors, then comes down* R.C.) Yes—it's better for you to hear this from me than to have to learn it for yourself. (*Sits on bench* R.C.) Clarence, women aren't the angels that you think they are. Well, now—first, let me explain this to you. You see, Clarence, we men have to run this world and it's not an easy job. It takes work, and it takes thinking. A man has to be sure of his facts and figures. He has to reason things out. Now you take a woman—a woman thinks—no I'm wrong right there—she doesn't think at all. She just gets stirred up. And she gets stirred up about the damnedest things. (*Remembering his own troubles*) Now, I love my wife just as much as any man, but that doesn't mean I should stand for a lot of folderol. (*Looks toward arch, exploding*) By God, I won't stand for it.

CLARENCE. Stand for what, Father?

FATHER. (*To himself*) That is one thing I shall not submit myself to. (*Turns to* CLARENCE) Clarence, if a man thinks a certain thing is the wrong thing to do he shouldn't do it. If he thinks it's right, he should do it. But that has nothing to do with whether he loves his wife or not.

CLARENCE. Who says it has, Father?

FATHER. They do.

CLARENCE. Who, sir?

FATHER. Women. They get stirred up—and they try to get you stirred up, too—but don't you let them, Clarence. As long as you can keep reason and logic in the argument,—no matter what it's about, a man can hold his own, of course. But if they can switch you—pretty soon the argument's about whether you love them or not. I swear I don't know how they do it. Don't you let 'em, Clarence, don't you let 'em.

CLARENCE. I see what you mean so far, Father. If you don't watch yourself, love can make you do a lot of things you don't want to do.

FATHER. Exactly.

CLARENCE. (*With new knowledge*) But if you do watch out and know just how to handle women—

FATHER. Then you'll be all right. All a man has to do is be firm. You know how at times I have to be firm with your Mother. (*Looks again toward arch*) Just now about this month's household accounts—

CLARENCE. But, Father, what can you do when they cry?

FATHER. (*Thinks for a second*) Well, that's quite a question. —You just have to make them understand that what you're doing is for their good. (*Turns back to* CLARENCE)

CLARENCE. I see.

FATHER. (*Rising and putting hand on son's shoulder*) Now, Clarence,—you know *all* about women. (FATHER *goes to* L. *of table and sits down in front of his account-book. He puts on his glasses, opens book and begins to sort bills.*) (CLARENCE *rises and looks at him*)

CLARENCE. (*Rather diffidently*) But, Father—

FATHER. Yes, Clarence.

CLARENCE. (*To* R. *of table*) I thought you were going to tell me about—?

FATHER. About what?

CLARENCE. About—women.

FATHER. (*After a pause—he suddenly understands to what* CLARENCE *is referring*) Clarence, there are some things gentlemen don't discuss! I've told you all you need to know. The thing for you to remember is—be firm! (*There is a knock at door*) Yes, come in. (MARY *opens the door and enters*)

MARY. Excuse me! (*She comes down* C., *looks* R., *then* L., *sees her handkerchief, goes to couch, picks it up and continues around* L. *side of couch*) (CLARENCE *crosses back of table to* U.L. *of* C. *to meet her, acting firm and dominating*) (MARY *passes below him without a glance*) (CLARENCE *wilts, then again assuming firmness, turns up in arch in an attempt to quail* MARY *with a look*) (MARY *marches upstairs, ignoring him*) (CLARENCE *turns back into room, defeated. He looks down at*

*his clothes unhappily, then decides to be firm with his father.
He straightens up and steps toward him. At this moment*
FATHER, *staring at a bill, emits his cry of rage*)

FATHER. Oh, God! (CLARENCE *retreats above table, then goes
slowly to window*) (*We hear door slam up-stairs and sound of*
VINNIE's *feet as she comes rushing down stairs to down* C.)

VINNIE. What's the matter, Clare? What's wrong?

FATHER. (*Rises, picking up bill*) I will not send this person
a cheque. (VINNIE *takes bill*) (FATHER *sits again*)

VINNIE. (*Looking at bill*) Why, Clare, that's the only hat I've
bought since March, and it was reduced from forty dollars.

FATHER. I don't question your buying the hat or what you
paid for it, but the person from whom you bought it—(*He
rises and takes bill from* VINNIE) This Mlle. Mimi—isn't fit to
be in the hat business, or any other.

VINNIE. I never went there before, but it's a very nice place
and I don't see why you object to it.

FATHER. I object to it because this confounded person doesn't
put her name on her bills! Mimi what? Mimi O'Brien? Mimi
Jones? Mimi Weinstein?

VINNIE. How do I know? It's just Mimi.

FATHER. It can't be just Mimi. She must have some other
name, confound it! I wouldn't make out a check payable to
Charley or Jimmy, and I will not make out a check payable
to *Mimi*. Find out what her last name is, and I'll pay her the
money. (*Sits down again*)

VINNIE. All right, Clare. All right. (*She starts out—slowly at
first—then tries to hurry. She gets up about two steps*)

FATHER. Just a minute, Vinnie, that isn't all.

VINNIE. But Clare, dear, Cora will be leaving any minute.

FATHER. Never mind Cora.

VINNIE. And it isn't polite for me—

FATHER. Never mind Cora. Sit down, Vinnie. (*He points to
chair* R. *of table*) Sit down. (VINNIE *crosses back of table
slowly—taking a peep at account-book as she passes. She then
sits* R. *of it*) (CLARENCE *goes slowly into hall, looks upstairs*)
Vinnie, you know I like to live well, and I want my family
to live well. But this house must be run on a sound business
basis. (VINNIE *has heard this before*) I must know how much
money I am spending and what for. (*Something out the win-*

59

dow attracts her attention) Now for instance, if you recall a week ago I gave you six dollars to buy a new coffee pot.

VINNIE. (*Quickly turning to him*) Yes, because you broke the old one. You threw it right on the floor.

FATHER. I'm not talking about that. I'm merely endeavoring—

VINNIE. And it was so silly to break that nice coffee-pot, Clare; there was nothing the matter with the coffee that morning. It was made just the same as always.

FATHER. It was not! It was made in a damned barbaric manner! (CLARENCE *disappears off* L.)

VINNIE. And besides, I couldn't get another imported one. That little shop has stopped selling them. They said the tariff wouldn't let them. And that's your fault, Clare, because you're always voting to raise the tariff.

FATHER. The tariff protects America against cheap foreign labor. Now I find among my bills—

VINNIE. The tariff does nothing but raise the prices and that's hard on everybody, especially the farmer. (*She sounds as though she is quoting*)

FATHER. (*Annoyed*) I wish to God you wouldn't talk about things you don't know a damn thing about!

VINNIE. I do too know about them. Miss Gulick says every intelligent woman should have some opinion—

FATHER. Who, may I ask, is Miss Gulick?

VINNIE. Why, Clare, you know, she's that current events woman I told you about, and the tickets are a dollar every Tuesday.

FATHER. Do you mean to tell me that a pack of idle-minded females pay a dollar apiece to listen to another female? Listen to me if you want to know anything about the events of the day.

VINNIE. But you get so excited, Clare, and besides, Miss Gulick says that our President, whom you're always belittling, prays to God for guidance and—

FATHER. (*Having had enough of Miss Gulick*) Vinnie, what happened to that six dollars?

VINNIE. What six dollars?

FATHER. I gave you six dollars to buy a new coffee-pot and now I find that you apparently got one at Lewis and Conger's and charged it. Here's their bill. "One coffee-pot—five dollars."

VINNIE. (*Quickly*) So you owe me a dollar and you can hand it right over. (*Holds out her hand for it*)

FATHER. I'll do nothing of the kind. What did you do with that six dollars?

VINNIE. Why Clare, I can't tell you now, dear. Why didn't you ask me at the time?

FATHER. Oh, my God!

VINNIE. Wait a moment! I spent four dollars and a half for that new umbrella I told you I wanted and you said I didn't need it but I did, very much.

FATHER. Now we are getting somewhere. (*He takes his pencil and writes in the account-book*) One umbrella—four dollars and fifty cents.

VINNIE. And that must have been the time I paid Mrs. Tobin for two extra days' washing.

FATHER. (*Writing*) Mrs. Tobin.

VINNIE. That's two dollars more.

FATHER. (*Still writing*) Two dollars.

VINNIE. That makes—six dollars—and fifty cents. That's another fifty cents you owe me.

FATHER. I don't owe you anything. What you owe me is an explanation of where my money's gone to! Now, we're going over this account-book—item by item.

VINNIE. I do the best I can to keep down expenses. And you know yourself that Cousin Phoebe spends twice as much as we do. (CLARENCE *enters from* L.—*looks upstairs, then sits on third step. He is very despondent*)

FATHER. Damn Cousin Phoebe—I don't wish to be told how she throws her money around!

VINNIE. Oh, Clare, how can you? And I thought you were so fond of Cousin Phoebe.

FATHER. I *am* fond of Cousin Phoebe, but I can do without hearing so much about her.

VINNIE. You talk about your own relatives enough.

FATHER. (*Hurt*) That's not fair, Vinnie. When I talk about my relatives I criticize them.

VINNIE. Of course, if I can't even speak of Cousin Phoebe—

FATHER. (*Loudly*) You can speak of her all you want to—but I won't have Cousin Phoebe or anyone else dictating to me

61

how to run my house. Now this month's total—

VINNIE. (*Righteously*) I didn't say a word about her dictating—

FATHER. (*Sputters*) You said—you—

VINNIE. Why, Clare—she isn't that kind.

FATHER. (*Dazed*) I swear, I don't know what you said now. (*Firmly*) You never stick to the point. I endeaver to show you how to run this house on a business basis, and you always wind up by jibbering and jabbering about everything else under the sun. Now there is a little item here of thirty-two dollars—

VINNIE. (*Distressed*) I don't know what you expect of me. I tire myself out chasing up and down those stairs all day long—trying to look after your comfort—to bring up our children—I do the mending and the marketing—as if that isn't enough, you expect me to be an expert book-keeper, too. (*She begins to cry*)

FATHER. (*Distressed*) Vinnie, I have no wish to be unreasonable,—but don't you understand I'm doing this for your good? (VINNIE *gives him a look, then with a wail—rises and crosses to window*) (FATHER *drops bills—then pencil on table—snaps off his glasses and swings chair so he faces front*) (*Helplessly*) I suppose I'll have to go ahead just paying the bills and hoping I've got money enough in the bank to meet them. (VINNIE *crosses to back of table*) But it's all very discouraging.

VINNIE. (*Repentantly*) I'll try to do better, Clare.

FATHER. (*Holds his hand out to her*) (*Affectionately*) That's all I'm asking. (VINNIE *goes to just R. of back of his chair. She puts her arm around his neck*) I'll go down and make out the checks and sign them. (VINNIE *doesn't seem entirely consoled, so he attempts a lighter note to cheer her up*) Oh, Vinnie, maybe I haven't any right to sign those checks? (*She looks at him*) Since in the sight of the Lord I haven't any name at all. (*He laughs loudly at his own joke*) (VINNIE *taking it seriously moves to L. of his chair*) Do you suppose the banks would feel that way about it, too—or do you think they'll take a chance?

VINNIE. That's right, Clare, to make those checks good, you'll have to be baptized.

FATHER. The bank doesn't care whether I've been baptized or

62

not. (*He starts to pick up bills*)

VINNIE. Well, I care. No matter what Dr. Lloyd says, I'm not sure we're really married—

FATHER. (*Sorry he started it*) Damn it, Vinnie, we have four children! If we're not married now, we never will be.

VINNIE. Oh, Clare, don't you see how serious this is? You've got to do something about it!

FATHER. (*Rises, with bills in his hand*) Well, right now I've got to do something about these damn bills you've run up. (*Sternly*) I'm going downstairs. (*Turns to pick up book, putting bills and pencil in it*)

VINNIE. Not before you give me that dollar and a half.

FATHER. (*Turning to her, astonished*) What dollar and a half?

VINNIE. The dollar and a half you owe me.

FATHER. I don't owe you any dollar and a half. I gave you some money to buy a coffee-pot for *me* and somehow it turned into an umbrella for *you*.

VINNIE. Clarence Day, what kind of a man are you? Quibbling about a dollar and a half when your immortal soul is in danger! (*Religion again—so* FATHER *turns away*) And what's more—

FATHER. (*Quickly*) All right. All right. All right. (*He takes three fifty-cent pieces from his change purse and gives them to her, one at a time, then puts purse back in his pocket*)

VINNIE. Thank you, Clare. There! Now the accounts are all straight again. (VINNIE *flounces out and upstairs*) (CLARENCE *rises to let her pass*) (FATHER *watches her go in astonishment, then gathers up his papers and book and starts out* C. *towards* L.)

CLARENCE. Father—you never did tell me—may I have a new suit of clothes?

FATHER. No, Clarence! (*Starts to go, then turns back*) I'm sorry, Clarence, but I have to be firm with you, too! (*He stalks off* L.) (JOHN *comes quickly down stairs, carrying a bag, which he takes out toward front door*) (CLARENCE *moves in to* U.L. *of* C.) (JOHN *returns empty-handed and starts up stairs again*)

CLARENCE. (*Getting an idea—turns up and takes* JOHN's *arm*) John, come here a minute.

JOHN. What do you want?

CLARENCE. (*Pulling him farther into room* C.) John, have you got any money you could lend me?

JOHN. With this week's allowance I'll have about—three dollars.

CLARENCE. That's no good. I've got to have enough to buy a new suit of clothes.

JOHN. Why don't you earn some money? That's what I'm going to do. I'm going to buy a bicycle—one of those new low kinds, with both wheels the same size—you know, a safety.

CLARENCE. How are you going to earn that much?

JOHN. I've got a job—practically. Look, I found this ad in the paper. (*Takes clipping from his pocket*) "Wanted, an energetic young man to handle household necessity that sells on sight. Liberal commissions—apply—

CARENCE. Liberal commissions? (*Takes clipping from* JOHN *and reads hurriedly*) "Apply 312 West 14th Street, Tuesday from eight to twelve." Listen John, let me have that job.

JOHN. (*Takes clipping*) Why should I give you my job? (*Crosses to* R.C.) They're hard to get.

CLARENCE. (*Following him*) But I've got to have a new suit of clothes.

JOHN. Maybe I could get a job for both of us? (*Doorbell rings vigorously*) I'll tell you what I'll do. I'll ask the man.

FATHER. (*Enters—calls up stairs*) Cora! Vinnie, that cab's here. Hurry up! (FATHER *goes toward front door*)

CLARENCE. John, we've both got to get down there early Tuesday—the first thing.

JOHN. Oh, no you don't—I'm going alone.

CLARENCE. But, John—

JOHN. But I'll put in a good word with the boss about you.

FATHER. (*Off* R.) They'll be right out. (CLARENCE *crosses quickly to* L. *We hear* FATHER *close front door*) Cora! Vinnie! (*He comes back to foot of stairs and calls up*) Are you coming? The cab's waiting.

VINNIE. (*From upstairs*) We heard you, Clare. We'll be down in a minute. (FATHER *comes into room*)

FATHER. John, go upstairs and hurry them down. (JOHN *goes upstairs*) (FATHER *crosses back of table to window and looks out, consulting his watch*) What's the matter with those women? Don't they know cabs cost money?—Clarence, go see what's causing this infernal delay. (CLARENCE *hurries up hall*) (MARY *comes sedately downstairs*)

CLARENCE. Here they come, Father. (FATHER *crosses quickly to back of table*) (CORA *and* VINNIE *follow* MARY *downstairs*) (MARY *passes* CLARENCE *without a glance and goes to* FATHER) (CLARENCE *goes to front of sofa*)

MARY. (*Extending her hand above table*) Goodbye, Mr. Day. I can't tell you how much I appreciate your hospitality.

FATHER. (*Shaking her hand and trying to hurry her*) Not at all! Not at all! (VINNIE *and* CORA *come into room*) (JOHN *comes downstairs with another bag and exits* R.)

CORA. Goodbye, Clarence. (*Starts toward* D.L.—*putting on gloves*)

FATHER. (*Crosses to* C. *quickly*) Cora, we can say good-bye to you on the sidewalk. (MARY *moves to* R. *upper corner of table*)

VINNIE. (R. *of* FATHER) There's no hurry—their train doesn't go until one-thirty. (*She crosses back of table to* MARY)

FATHER. Cabs cost money. If they have any waiting to do they should do it at Grand Central Depot. They've got a waiting-room there, it's just *for* that.

VINNIE. (*To* MARY) If there's one thing Mr. Day can't stand it's to keep a cab waiting.

CORA. It's been so nice seeing you again, Clarence. (*She kisses him*)—I hope—(*No one is in a hurry except* FATHER, *and it annoys him*) (MARGARET *enters with a box of lunch*)

MARGARET. (*Starting down to* CORA) Here's the lunch.

FATHER. All right. All right. Give it to me . . . Let's get started. (*He takes it from* MARGARGET—*and starts* U.C.) (MAR-GARET *follows* FATHER *up—then exits* C. *to* L.)

CORA. (*Starting up*) Where's John? (VINNIE *goes to* CORA)

FATHER. (*As he is leaving room*) He's outside. Come on. (CORA *and* VINNIE *follow, ad libbing goodbyes, ect.*) (MARY *starts, crosses below table to* C. *as* CORA *and* VINNIE *exit*)

CLARENCE. (*Crosses to* C.) Mary—aren't you going to—shake hands with me?

MARY. I don't think I'd better. You may remember that when I get too close to you, you feel contaminated. (*She starts* U.C.)

CLARENCE. (*Follows her*) Mary, you're going to write to me, aren't you?

MARY. Are you going to write first?

CARENCE. (*Facing front very much his* FATHER) No, Mary—

65

there are times when a man must be firm. (JOHN *enters hurriedly*)

JOHN. Mary, Mother says you'd better hurry out before Father starts yelling. It's Sunday. (MARY *crosses back of* JOHN—*then turns back to him—offering her hand—which he takes*)

MARY. Goodbye, John. I'm very happy to have made your acquaintance. (SHE *walks out*) (CLARENCE *is crushed*) (JOHN *gives* CLARENCE *a questioning look—grins—and follows her*) (CLARENCE *dashes into arch; just then we hear door slam. For a moment* CLARENCE'S *world has fallen about him—but he decides quickly and rushes to side table* U.R.C., *takes a pad of writing paper and a pencil from drawer—rushes to* L. *of table, sits and starts to write—in desperation*)

CLARENCE. "Dear Mary"—

QUICK CURTAIN

ACT TWO

Scene 2

SCENE: *The same.*

Two days later. The breakfast table.

The bowl of fruit is on side table U.R.C. *Dishes and silverware have been removed from* JOHN'S *place. The fruit is ready at* FATHER'S *and* CLARENCE'S *places. There are two cups of coffee and the sugar-bowl on side table* U.R.C.

HARLAN *and* WHITNEY *are at table, ready to start breakfast. Their glasses of milk are in front of them.*

CLARENCE *is near window, reading newspaper.*

NORA, *a new maid,—heavily built and along towards middle age,—is just entering, carrying two plates and bowls of cereal. She serves* HARLAN, *then* WHITNEY. *As she puts cereal in front of* WHITNEY *the postman's whistle blows twice and door-bell rings.*

NORA *starts toward* C., *front of table.*

CLARENCE *glances out window.*

CLARENCE. Never mind, Nora. It's the postman—I'll go. (*He runs out through arch and exits toward outside door, putting*

66

paper at FATHER's *place as he goes*) (NORA *crosses* U.R. *of table*)

WHITNEY. (*To* NORA) You forgot the sugar. It goes here between me and Father.

NORA. Oh, yes. (NORA *gets sugar-bowl from side table* U.R.C.—*puts it near* FATHER's *place, then waits* U.R.) (*We hear front door slam*) (CLARENCE *comes back with three or four letters which he looks through quickly, and then his face falls in utter dejection—moves to back of table*) (FATHER *comes down stairs*)

FATHER. Good morning, boys! (CLARENCE *crosses to his chair at table—*BOYS *rise.* ALL *say "Good morning, Sir."*) (FATHER *comes into room*) John not down yet? (*He shouts upstairs*) John! Hurry down to your breakfast.

CLARENCE. John had his breakfast early, Father, and went out to see about something.

FATHER. See about what?

CLARENCE. John and I thought we'd work this summer and earn some money.

FATHER. (*Crosses to his place at table*) Good! Sit down, boys. (*The two young* BOYS *sit. They use cream and sugar on cereal and put them near* FATHER's *place again*)

CLARENCE. We saw an ad in the paper and John went down to see about it.

FATHER. Why didn't you go, too? (NORA *crosses to* U.L.C.—*awaits orders*)

CLARENCE. I was expecting an answer to a letter I wrote, but it didn't come. (FATHER *sits*) Here's the mail. (*Puts mail* L. *of* FATHER) (*He seems depressed, but sits and starts to eat*)

FATHER. (*Takes his napkin and spreads it on his lap*) What kind of work is this you're planning to do?

CLARENCE. Sort of salesman, the ad said.

FATHER. (*Eating his fruit*) Un-hum. Work never hurt anybody. It's good for them. But if you're going to work—work hard. King Solomon had the right idea about work. (BOYS *stop eating and look at* FATHER.) "Whatever thy hand findeth to do," Solomon said, "Do thy damnedest."—Where's your mother? (*The* BOYS *start eating again*)

NORA. If you please, sir, Mrs. Day doesn't want any breakfast. She isn't feeling well so she went back upstairs to lie down again.

FATHER. Now why does your mother do that to me? She knows when she doesn't come down to breakfast she just upsets my whole day . . . Clarence, go tell your mother I'll be up to see her before I start for the office.

CLARENCE. (*Rises*) Yes, sir. (*He goes upstairs*)

HARLAN. What's the matter with Mother?

FATHER. There's nothing the matter with your mother. Perfectly healthy woman.—Whenever she gets an ache or a twinge, instead of being firm about it, she just gives in to it. (*Doorbell rings, then post-man's whistle blows once.*) (NORA *answers it.*) Boys, after breakfast, you find out what your mother wants you to do today. Whitney, you take care of Harlan. (NORA *comes back with special delivery letter on salver. Letter and envelope are of pink paper*)

WHITNEY. Yes, Father.

NORA. (*Impressed*) It's a special delivery, sir.

FATHER. (*Taking letter*) Thank you. (*He takes letter out and puts envelope to his* L.—*then gets out his glasses and starts to read letter*) (NORA *takes salver to off* C. *to* R. *then crosses to arch and exits* C. *to* L.) (*Then* CLARENCE *comes rushing down stairs*)

CLARENCE. Was that the postman again?

WHITNEY. It was a special delivery.

CLARENCE. (*To back of table*) Yes? Where is it?

WHITNEY. It was for Father.

CLARENCE. (*Again disappointed*) Oh—(*He sits at table*) (FATHER *is having trouble with letter. He turns it over and looks at signature, then looks back to first page, then gives a shrug and settles down to read it.—Before he has finished half the first page he says—*)

FATHER. I don't understand this at all. Here's a letter from some woman I never heard of. (*He goes on reading*) (CLARENCE *sees envelope, picks it up, looks at postmark, realizes that it's from* MARY—*He is worried*)

CLARENCE. (*Rises*) Father—

FATHER. (*Exploding*) Oh, God!

CLARENCE. What is it, Father?

FATHER. This woman claims that she sat on my lap. (CLARENCE *begins to feel uncomfortable*) (FATHER *goes on reading a little further, then holds letter over in front of* CLARENCE) What's

68

that word? (CLARENCE *begins feverishly to read as much as possible, but* FATHER *cuts in after a moment*) No, that word down here. (*He points*)

CLARENCE. It looks like—"curiosity." (FATHER *withdraws letter*) (CLARENCE's *eyes follow it hungrily*)

FATHER. (*Reading*) "I opened your letter only as a matter of curiosity." (*He turns page*)

CLARENCE. (*In agony, after a painful moment of hoping* FATHER *will continue to read out loud*) Yes? Go on.

FATHER. This gets worse and worse! Just turns into a lot of sentimental lovey-dovey mush. (*He rises and crushes letter, then crosses to* L.) (VINNIE *hurries down stairs. She is dressed in a negligee. Her hair is in braids*) Is this someone's idea of a practical joke?

VINNIE. (*As she comes down stairs*) What's the matter, Clare!

FATHER. I don't know why I should always be the butt— (*Throws letter in fire place*)

VINNIE. (*Entering room*) What's wrong! (*The* CHILDREN *rise as* MOTHER *enters*)

FATHER. (*Crosses up behind sofa to her. He puts his glasses away*) Nothing wrong—just a damn fool letter. How are you, Vinnie?

VINNIE. I don't feel well, Clare. I thought you needed me, but if you don't, I'll go back to bed.

FATHER. (*Drawing her down and putting her in her chair*) Well, now that you're here, sit down and have some breakfast with us. Sit down, Vinnie. Sit down. (VINNIE *sits, very reluctantly and protesting*) (CHILDREN *sit*) (NORA *enters* C. *from* R. *with a tray of bacon and eggs, goes to side of table* U.L.C.) Get some food in your stomach. Do you good.

VINNIE. I don't feel like eating anything, Clare.

FATHER. (*Heartily*) That's all the more reason why you should eat. Build up your strength. (NORA *is* U.L.C. *at side table, her back turned toward* FATHER) (*He addresses her*) Here-re-re— (*To* CLARENCE) What's this one's name?

CLARENCE. (*Sits*) Nora.

FATHER. Nora! Some bacon and eggs to Mrs. Day. (*He crosses back of table to his chair and sits*)

VINNIE. No, Clare! (NORA *however has gone to Vinnie's side with platter*) No, take it away, Nora. I don't even want to

69

smell it. (*During following,* NORA *puts platter of bacon and eggs on side table* U.R.C., *then removes fruit from* FATHER *and* CLARENCE, *places them* U.R.C. *Picks up bacon and eggs and serves* FATHER, *replaces bacon and eggs* U.R.C. *Picks up two cups of coffee—serves* FATHER, *then* CLARENCE, *then gets bacon and eggs again and serves* CLARENCE. *Then puts platter on tray on side table* U.L.C. *After that she takes remains of fruit from side table* U.R.C.—*Crosses to side table* U.L.C.—*puts them on tray, then takes tray and exits* C. *to* L.)

FATHER. Vinnie, it's just weak to give in to an ailment. Any disease can be cured by firmness. What you need is strength of character.

VINNIE. (*With sick protest*) I don't know why you object to my complaining a little. I notice when you have a headache you yell and groan and swear enough.

FATHER. Of course I yell. (*Picks up serving-spoon and fork*) That's to prove to the headache that I'm stronger than it is— (*Helping himself to bacon and eggs*) I can generally swear one right out of my system.

VINNIE. This isn't a headache. I think I've caught some kind of a germ. There's a lot of sickness around. Several of my friends have had to send for the doctor. I may have the same thing. (WHITNEY *finishes breakfast—puts napkin in ring*)

FATHER. (*He uses cream and sugar—passes them to* CLARENCE) Vinnie, I'll bet this is all your imagination. You hear of a lot of other people having some disease and you get scared and think you have it yourself. So you take to your bed and send for the doctor. The doctor—all poppycock!

VINNIE. I didn't say a word about my sending for the doctor.

FATHER. I should hope not. Doctors think they know a damn lot but they don't. (HARLAN *finishes—puts napkin in ring*)

VINNIE. But Clare, dear, when people are seriously ill you have to do something.

FATHER. Certainly you have to do something! Cheer 'em up— that's the way to cure 'em!

VINNIE. (*With slight irony*) How would you go about cheering them up?

FATHER. I? I'd tell 'em—bah! (VINNIE, *out of exasperation and weakness begins to cry*) (FATHER *looks at her amazed*) What have I done now?

VINNIE. (*Rises and moves to* C.) Oh, Clare—hush up! (HARLAN *slides out of his chair and runs over to her at* C. *and puts his arms around her*) Harlan, dear, keep away from Mother. You might catch what she's got. Whitney—(*She goes to sofa and sits—*L. *end of it*)

WHITNEY. (*Rises, crosses to above* HARLAN *at* C.) Yes, Mother.

VINNIE. If you have finished your breakfast—I promised Mrs. Whitehead to send over Margaret's recipe for Floating Island Pudding. Margaret has it all written out. And take Harlan with you.

WHITNEY. (*Sympathetically*) All right, Mother. I hope you feel better. (WHITNEY *takes* HARLAN's *hand and leads him out* C. *to* L. HARLAN *keeps his eyes on Mother as long as he can*) (FATHER *goes over and sits beside* VINNIE *on sofa, speaking as he goes*) (CLARENCE *also has finished and puts napkin in ring and sits very quietly*)

FATHER. Vinnie. (*Contritely*) I didn't mean to upset you. I was just trying to help! (*Pats her hand*) When you take to your bed I have a damned lonely time around here. So when I see you getting it into your head that you're sick, I want to do something about it. (*Continues to pat her hand. He gets very hale and hearty. His hand-pats become vigorous*) Now Vinnie, just because some of your friends have given in to this is no reason why you should imagine you're sick—

VINNIE. (*Snatches her hand away*) Oh! Stop, Clare!—Get out of this house and go to your office! (FATHER *is a little bewildered and somewhat indignant at this rebuff to his feelings of tenderness. He gets up and goes out into hall to* L.—*a moment later with his hat and stick, he marches across arch and out of house, slamming door*) (VINNIE *gets up after door slams and starts toward arch*)

CLARENCE. (*Rises and goes to her* L. *of* C.) I'm sorry you're not feeling well, Mother.

VINNIE. I'll be all right, Clarence. Remember I had a touch of this last Fall and I was all right the next morning.

CLARENCE. Are you sure you don't want the doctor?

VINNIE. Oh, no. I really don't need him—and besides, doctors worry your father. I don't want him to be upset. (*She starts up again*)

CLARENCE. (*Following her*) Is there anything I can do for you?

VINNIE. (*Stops* U.C.) Ask Margaret to send me a cup of tea. I'll try to drink it. I'm going back to bed. (*She starts up stairs*)

CLARENCE. (*At foot of stairs*) Do you mind if John and I go out today, or will you need us?

VINNIE. You run along. I just want to be left alone. (*She exits top of stairs*) (CLARENCE *starts for the fire place eager to retrieve* MARY's *letter*) (NORA *enters with a tray to clear table.* HE *stops*)

CLARENCE. (*Back of sofa*) Oh!—Nora—will you take a cup of tea up to Mrs. Day in her room?

NORA. Yes sir. (NORA *exits*) (*Then* CLARENCE *hurries to fire place, gets crumpled letter and starts to read it feverishly. He reads quickly then draws a deep, happy breath. Door slams. He puts letter in his pocket*) (*We see* JOHN's *hat fly by arch, to* L., *and hear the whistling sound*) (JOHN *enters, carrying two heavy packages which he puts on* C. *of breakfast table*)

CLARENCE. (*Crosses below sofa to* C.) Did you get the job?

JOHN. Yes, for both of us. Look, I got it with me.

CLARENCE. What is it?

JOHN. (*Unwrapping top of one package*) Medicine.

CLARENCE. (*Dismayed*) Medicine! You took a job for us to go out and sell medicine!

JOHN. But it's *wonderful* medicine. (JOHN *gets a bottle out of package. He reads from bottle*) "Bartlett's Beneficent Balm —a Boon to Mankind." Look what it cures! (*He hands bottle to* CLARENCE, *who reads from label*)

CLARENCE. "A sovereign cure for colds, coughs, catarrah, asthma, quinsy and sore throat;—(*Moves to below sofa—*JOHN *follows him*) poor digestion, summer complaint, colic, dys pepsia, heart-burn, and shortness of breath;—lumbago, rheu matism, heart disease, giddiness, and woman's complaints;— nervous prostration, St. Vitus' Dance, jaundice and la grippe; proud flesh, pink eye, seasickness, and pimples." (*As* CLAR- ENCE *reads off list he has become more and more impressed, with occasional looks, toward* JOHN, *of growing confidence*)

JOHN. See?

CLARENCE. That sounds all right!

JOHN. It's made "from a secret formula known only to Dr. Bartlett."

CLARENCE. He must be quite a doctor.

JOHN. (*Enthusiastically*) It sells for a dollar a bottle! And we get twenty-five cents' commission on every bottle.

CLARENCE. Where does he want us to sell it?

JOHN. He's given us the territory of all Manhattan Island.

CLARENCE. That's bully. Anybody that's sick at all ought to need a bottle of this. (*Hands bottle to* JOHN *and crosses to* C. *toward package*) Let's start by calling on friends of Father and Mother.

JOHN. That's a good idea. But wait a minute. Suppose they ask us if we used it at our house.

CLARENCE. (*Steps* C.) Oh, yes, it would be better if we could say we did. (NORA *enters with tray on which is a cup of tea and a napkin. She goes to table, puts tray on* L. *end of it—crosses to* R. *of table to get sugar bowl and cream pitcher, which she puts on tray*)

JOHN. But we can't because we haven't had it here long enough.

CLARENCE. Is that the tea for Mrs. Day?

NORA. Yes.

CLARENCE. I'll take it up to her. You needn't bother.

NORA. Thank you. Take it up right away while it's good and hot. (*She exits* C. *to* L.)

CLARENCE. (*Forgetting about medicine and concerned about* MOTHER) Mother wasn't feeling well this morning.

JOHN. (*Sympathetically*) What was the matter with her?

CLARENCE. I don't know—she was just complaining.

JOHN. (*Getting an idea—consulting bottle, quickly—crosses to* CLARENCE) Well, it says here it's good for *women's complaints.* (THEY *look at each other a second;* CLARENCE *takes bottle with his* L. *hand—takes out cork and smells it.* JOHN *pulls* CLARENCE's *hand toward him so that he also can smell it.* THEY *look at each other—*JOHN *nods.* CLARENCE *crosses to table and picks up spoon with* R. *hand pours medicine into it. He hands bottle back to* JOHN *puts medicine in tea and starts to stir tea.* JOHN *holds bottle a second—looks at it—then suddenly pours some more of medicine into tea. Quick curtain*)

(*The* CURTAIN *is lowered for a few seconds to denote a lapse of three hours*)

(*When Curtain rises again breakfast things have been cleared and the room is in order. The bowl of fruit again on table.*

VINNIE'S *prayer book is on mantel*) (HARLAN *is kneeling on* FATHER'S *armchair, looking out window as if watching for somebody*) (MARGARET *enters hurriedly down the stairs*)
MARGARET. Has your father come yet?
HARLAN. Not yet.
MARGARET. Glory be—(NORA *enters from downstairs with a steaming tea-kettle and a towel and* MARGARET *meets her at arch*) Hurry that upstairs. The doctor's waiting for it. (NORA *starts upstairs*) (MARGARET *goes to foot of stairs*) And Nora, see if there is anything else you can do! I've got to go out.
NORA. (*On third step*) Where are you going?
MARGARET. I have to go and get the minister. (NORA *goes up-stairs and exits*) (MARGARET *starts taking off her apron*)
HARLAN. There's a cab coming up the street.
MARGARET. Well, I hope it's him, poor man—but a cab doesn't sound like your Father. (*She exits* L., *downstairs*) (HARLAN *watches, then runs to downstairs staircase, and kneels as he yells downstairs*)
HARLAN. Yes, it's Father. Whitney got him all right. (HARLAN *runs back toward chair—but stops* R.C.—*front of table, when front door slams*) (FATHER *crosses arch, and runs upstairs*) (WHITNEY *comes into arch and down* C. *He is very pleased with himself*) What took you so long?
WHITNEY. (D.C.) Long? I wasn't long. I went right down on the elevated, and got Father right away and we came all the way back in a cab.
HARLAN. I thought you were never coming.
WHITNEY. Well, the horse didn't go very fast at first. The cabby whipped him and swore at him and still he wouldn't gallop. Then Father spoke to the horse. (*Very pleased with himself, he rocks on his feet and swings his hat for a few seconds*)—How is Mother?
HARLAN. I don't know. The doctor's up there now.
WHITNEY. (*Crossing* L.) Well, she'd better be good and sick or Father may be mad at me for getting him up here—(*Stops and turns quickly*) Especially in a *cab*.
FATHER. (*From up stairs*) Damn! Damnation! (*We hear a door slam and* FATHER'S *angry foot-steps as he comes down stairs and into the room*)
FATHER. (*Crossing* D.C., *then crosses* R., *then* U.R. *Indignantly*)

74

Well, huh!—It seems to me I ought to be shown a little consideration. I guess I've got some feelings, too!

WHITNEY. Father, Mother's awfully sick, isn't she?

FATHER. (*Crossing back of table toward arch*) How do I know? I wasn't allowed to stay in the same room with her!

WHITNEY. Father—who put you out, the doctor?

FATHER. (*In arch. Loudly*) No, it was your mother, damn it! (*He goes out* L. *and hangs up his hat and stick*) (WHITNEY *crosses* U.L. *of sofa and puts his hat on side table* U.L.C., *then goes to back of sofa*) (HARLAN *moves to* L. *of table,* R. *of* C.) (FATHER *returns. He may be annoyed, but he is also worried*) You boys keep quiet around here today. (*He paces to* R., *front of table*)

WHITNEY. (*Back of sofa. Hopefully*) Father, Mother must be pretty sick.

FATHER. She must be, Whitney. I don't know—I can only guess. (*Crosses to* L.) (DR. HUMPHREYS *comes down stairs, with his satchel. Stops on last step*) Nobody ever tells me anything in this house.

DR. HUMPHREYS. Mrs. Day is quieter now. (*Starts to exit*)

FATHER. Well, Doctor? (*Crossing to* L. *of* C.) How is Mrs. Day? What's the matter with her?

DR. HUMPHREYS. (*Crossing* D.C. *to* FATHER) She's a pretty sick woman, Mr. Day. I had given her a sedative—just before you arrived,—after you left the room I had to give her another.— Have you a telephone?

FATHER. A telephone! No—I don't believe in them. Why?

DR. HUMPHREYS. It would just have saved me a few steps. I'll be back in about ten minutes. (*He turns to go*)

FATHER. Just a minute—I think I'm entitled to know what's the matter with my wife? (DR. HUMPHREYS *turns back*)

DR. HUMPHREYS. What did Mrs. Day have for breakfast this morning?

FATHER. She didn't eat anything—not a thing.

DR. HUMPHREYS. Are you sure?

FATHER. I tried to get her to eat something, but she wouldn't.

DR. HUMPHREYS. (*Almost to himself*) I can't understand it.

FATHER. Understand what?

DR. HUMPHREYS. These violent attacks of nausea. It's almost as though she were poisoned.

75

FATHER. What?

DR. HUMPHREYS. (*Starts up* C.) I'll try not to be gone more than ten or fifteen minutes. (DR. HUMPHREYS *exits* C. *to* R.)

FATHER. (*Going* U.C.) But, see here—if you really—(*We hear street door close*) (*Angrily, trying to reassure himself, crosses* D.L.) Damn doctors! They never know what's the matter with anybody. (*Indignantly he crosses to window* D.R.) He'd better get your mother well and damn soon or he'll hear from me!

WHITNEY. (*Really worried about Mother now*) Father, Mother is going to get well, isn't she?

FATHER. (*The thought worries him for a moment*) Of course she's going to get well.

HARLAN. (*Running to* FATHER—*puts his arms around him*) I hope Mother gets well soon. When Mother stays in bed it's lonesome.

FATHER. Yes, it is, Harlan.—It's lonesome. (*With his arm around* HARLAN's *shoulder* THEY *move to* C. *When they stop,* HARLAN *is down-stage of* FATHER) What were you boys supposed to do today?

WHITNEY. (*Crosses* D.L.) I was to learn the rest of my catechism.

FATHER. (*Smoothing* HARLAN's *tie and collar*) Well, if that's what your mother wanted you to do, you'd better do it.

WHITNEY. (*Positively*) I know it. (*Then dubiously*) I think.

FATHER. You'd better be sure.

WHITNEY. I can't be sure unless somebody hears me—will you hear me?

FATHER. Yes, Whitney—yes, I'll hear you. (WHITNEY *goes to mantel and gets prayer book*) (FATHER *crosses to sofa and sits. Puts on his glasses*)

HARLAN. (*Follows him and sits beside* FATHER) If Mother is still sick will you read to me tonight?

FATHER. Of course I'll read to you. (*He pats* HARLAN's *knee and they laugh. He is going to enjoy these moments with his sons*) (WHITNEY *opens prayer book and hands it to* FATHER)

WHITNEY. Here it is, Father. Just the end of it. Mother knows I know the rest. Look, start here. (*Points to question, then steps back to* D.L.)

FATHER. (*So that his youngest son may also enjoy these moments with him,* FATHER *holds book so that* HARLAN *can look at it, and as* WHITNEY *finishes each answer* HARLAN *quickly*

76

looks up to FATHER *as if to say "Pretty good, Eh!")* (*Reading*) "How many parts are there in a Sacrament?"

WHITNEY. (*Reciting*) "Two: the outward visible sign, and the inward spiritual grace." (FATHER *nods in approval and smiles at* HARLAN)

FATHER. "What is the outward visible sign or form in Baptism?"

WHITNEY. "Water; wherein the person is baptized, in the Name of the Father and of the Son and of the Holy Ghost."— You haven't been baptized, Father, have you?

FATHER. (*Ignoring it*) "What is the inward and spiritual grace?"

WHITNEY. If you don't have to be baptized, why do I have to be confirmed?

FATHER. (*Rather sharply*) "What is the inward and spiritual grace?"

WHITNEY. "A death unto sin, and a new birth unto righteousness; for being by nature born in sin, and the children of wrath, we are hereby made the children of grace."—Is that why you get mad so much, Father—because you're a child of wrath?

FATHER. Whitney, mind your manners! You're not supposed to ask questions of your elders! (FATHER *isn't enjoying himself now*) "What is required of persons to be baptized?"

WHITNEY. (*A little frightened*) "Repentence, whereby"— whereby—

FATHER. You don't know it well enough, Whitney. (*He shuts book and hands it to him, sharply. Snaps off his glasses and crosses to* R.C.) You'd better study it some more.

WHITNEY. Now?

FATHER. No,—no, you don't have to do it now. (WHITNEY *puts book on mantel*) Let's see, now, what can we do?

WHITNEY. (*Crossing to* C.—*edging up towards arch*) I was working with my tool-chest out in the back yard. (HARLAN *rises as* WHITNEY *passes him*)

FATHER. Better not do any hammering with your mother sick upstairs. You'd better stay here.

WHITNEY. I wasn't hammering—I was doing wood carving.

FATHER. Well, Harlan—how about you—shall we play a game of tiddle-de-winks?

HARLAN. (*Moving up beside* WHITNEY) I was helping Whitney.
FATHER. Oh—all right. (*The* BOYS *start* U.C. *slowly—but as soon as* FATHER *looks away, they run and exit* C. *to* L.) (FATHER *goes to arch—calls down stairway softly*) Boys—Boys, don't do any shouting out there. We all have to be very quiet around here today. (*We hear Boys say "Yes, Father"*) (FATHER *stands in hall surveying room; looking and feeling very lonesome, then he looks up toward* VINNIE, *worried. Then he starts up stairs but changes his mind. Returns and goes to rail of basement stairs, and calls quietly*) Margaret! (*There is no answer and he raises his voice a little*) Margaret! (*Still no answer and he lets loose*) Margaret! Why don't you answer when you hear me calling? (*At this moment* MARGARET, *wearing hat and shawl appears in arch from* R., *having come through front door*) Mar—
MARGARET. Sh—sh—(FATHER *turns quickly and sees* MARGARET)
FATHER. Oh, there you are!
MARGARET. (*Reprovingly, but deferentially*) We must all be quiet, Mr. Day—Mrs. Day is very sick.
FATHER. (*Testily*) I know she's sick. That's what I wanted you for. You go up and wait outside her door in case she needs anything. (MARGARET *starts to go up*) (FATHER *swings to* MARGARET's *right—foot of stairs*) And what were you doing out of of the house, anyway?
MARGARET. (*On stairs*) I was sent for the minister.
FATHER. (*Startled*) The minister?
MARGARET. Yes, sir. He's outside now, paying off the cab. (FATHER *moves to* L. *side of arch*) (*Door offstage* R. *closes.* MARGARET *bows as if to the minister and exits upstairs*) (DR. LLOYD *appears in arch and goes to* FATHER, *offering his hand, which* FATHER *takes*)
DR. LLOYD. I was deeply shocked to hear of Mrs. Day's illness. I hope I can be of some service. Will you take me up to her?
FATHER. Mrs. Day is resting now and she can't be disturbed.
DR. LLOYD. But I've been summoned.
FATHER. (*After a moment's thought*) The doctor will be back in a few minutes and we'll see what he has to say about it. (*Another short pause.* FATHER *doesn't relish a visit with the minister but, of course, he is polite*) You'd better come in and wait.

DR. LLOYD. Thank you. (DR. LLOYD *comes into room and sits on bench* R.C. *Putting his hat on table* R.C.) Mrs. Day has been a tower of strength in the parish. Everyone liked her so much. Yes, she was a fine woman.

FATHER. (*At table* R. *of sofa*) I wish to God you wouldn't talk about Mrs. Day as if she were dead. (*He moves toward back of sofa*) (NORA *comes down stairs hurriedly*)

NORA. Mr. Day—Is the doctor back yet?

FATHER. (*Crossing to* R. *of arch*) No. Does she need him?

NORA. She's kind of restless, sir. She's talking in her sleep and twisting and turning. (*She exits* C. *to* L.)

FATHER. (*Looks upstairs—then off* R., *then crosses back of table to window*) That doctor said he'd be right back.

MARGARET. (*Coming downstairs*) The doctor's coming. I was watching for him out the window. (*She goes to front door*) (FATHER *crosses front of table, swings to* L. *of* C.) (*A moment later we hear* DR. HUMPHREYS *say, "Thank you Margaret."* DR. HUMPHREYS *enters, starts toward stairs*) (DR. LLOYD *rises*)

FATHER. (*At* L. *of* C.) Well, Doctor, seems to me that was a pretty long ten minutes. (DR. HUMPHREYS *enters room but stops short at* FATHER's *remark and tone*)

DR. HUMPHREYS. (*Coming* D.R. *of* C. *Testily*) See here, Mr. Day, if I'm to be responsible for Mrs. Day's health, I must be allowed to handle this case in my own way.

FATHER. Well, you can't handle it while you're out of the house. (MARGARET *shows on* DR. SOMERS, *who stops* U.C.) (MARGARET *exits up stairs*)

DR. HUMPHREYS. (*Flaring*) I left this house because—(*Seeing* DR. SOMERS) Mr. Day, this is Dr. *Somers*.

DR. SOMERS. (*Crossing to* FATHER—*offering his hand, which* FATHER *takes*) How do you do.

DR. HUMPHREYS. I felt that Mrs. Day's condition warranted getting Dr. Somers here as quickly as possible—for a consultation. I hope that meets with your approval?

FATHER. (*A little awed*) Why, yes, of course. Anything that can be done.

DR. HUMPHREYS. Upstairs, Doctor! (*The* TWO DOCTORS *go upstairs*) (FATHER *crosses* U. *to* R. *of arch, a little shaken*)

DR. LLOYD. Mrs. Day is in good hands now. There's nothing you and I can do at the moment to help.

FATHER. Dr. Lloyd—(*Crosses* D.R.C. *and indicates to* DR. LLOYD *to sit.* DR. LLOYD *sits on* R. *of bench*) There's something that's troubling Mrs. Day's mind. (*Sits on bench*) I think you know what I refer to. (FATHER *looks toward upstairs*)

DR. LLOYD. Yes—you mean the fact that you've never been baptized?

FATHER. (*Stormily turning on him*) I gathered you knew about it—from your sermon last Sunday. (FATHER *looks at him a second with indignant memory, then cools down*) But let's not get angry. I think something should be done about it.

DR. LLOYD. Yes, Mr. Day.

FATHER. When those doctors get through up there I want you to talk to Mrs. Day. I want you to tell her something.

DR. LLOYD. Yes, I'll be glad to.

FATHER. You're just the man to do it. She shouldn't be upset about this—and I want you to tell her that my being baptized would just be a lot of damned nonsense.

DR. LLOYD. But, Mr. Day!

FATHER. No, she'd take your word on a thing like that—and we've got to do everything we can to help her now.

DR. LLOYD. (*Rises*) Mr. Day, baptism is one of the sacraments of the church—

FATHER. (*Rises*) You're her minister and you're supposed to bring her comfort and peace of mind.

DR. LLOYD. The solution is so simple. It would take only your consent to be baptized.

FATHER. That's out of the question,—and I'm surprised that a grown man like you should suggest such a thing. (FATHER *crosses to* L.) (*The* DOCTORS *start down stairs*)

DR. LLOYD. (*Following him to* L.C.) If you're really concerned about Mrs. Day's peace of mind, don't you think—?

FATHER. Now see here—if—(*He turns so he sees the* DOCTORS *entering.* FATHER *crosses to* L. *of* C.—*meets* DR. HUMPHREYS) Well, Doctor, how is Mrs. Day? What have you decided?

DR. HUMPHREYS. (*At* R. *of* C.) Is there a room we could use for our consultation? (DR. SOMERS *has gone to back of table* R.C.)

FATHER. (*A little uneasy*) Of course. (MARGARET *comes downstairs*) (DR. HUMPHREYS *moves to* DR. SOMERS U.R.C.) (FATHER *moves up to* L. *of arch, the storm breaking on* MARGARET) Margaret!—you go back upstairs! I don't̊ want Mrs. Day left alone.

MARGARET. (*Still on stairs*) There is something I have to do for the Doctor. I'll go back up as soon as I get it started.

FATHER. Well, hurry. (MARGARET *comes down and starts toward* L., *but stops as* FATHER *speaks*) And, Margaret—show these—gentlemen—downstairs to the billiard room.

MARGARET. Yes, sir. This way, Doctors—please—downstairs. (MARGARET *exits, followed by* DR. SOMERS)

FATHER. (*As* DR. HUMPHREYS *starts to follow*) Dr. Humphreys, you know now, don't you—this isn't serious—is it?

DR. HUMPHREYS. After we've had our consultation, we'll talk to you, Mr. Day.

FATHER. (*Annoyed at being put off*) But surely you must—?

DR. HUMPHREYS. Rest assured Dr. Somers will do everything that is humanly possible. (*Crosses behind* FATHER, *exits* L.)

FATHER. (*Swinging to* C. *Now he is really very worried*) Why, —you don't mean—

DR. HUMPHREYS. (*Offstage*) We'll try not to be long. (FATHER *looks up stairs—then down lower stair-well—where Doctors have gone—as he looks up again he catches* DR. LLOYD's *eye*) (FATHER *is obviously frightened—but he tries not to show it*)

FATHER. (*Quietly*) This Dr. Somers—I've heard his name often —he's very well thought of, isn't he?

DR. LLOYD. Oh, yes, indeed. (D.L.)

FATHER. (*Comes* D.C.) If Vinnie's seriously—if anyone could help her, he could,—don't you think?

DR. LLOYD. A very fine physician. (FATHER, *very worried, looks away*) But there's a greater help, ever present in the hour of need. Let us turn to Him in prayer. Let us kneel and pray. (FATHER *looks at him, straightens up, walks to down* R. *side of room—then turns toward* DR. LLOYD) Let us kneel and pray. (*After a moment* FATHER *finally bows his head*) (DR. LLOYD *looks at him, astonished, and not kneeling himself, speaks simply in prayer*) Oh, Lord, look down from Heaven—behold, visit, and relieve this thy servant who is grieved with sickness, and extend unto her thy accustomed goodness. We know she has sinned against thee in thought, word, and deed. Have mercy on her, Oh Lord, have mercy on this miserable sinner. (FATHER *is annoyed*) Forgive her, Oh Lord—!

FATHER. (*Losing control*) She's not a miserable sinner and

81

you know it! (FATHER *now shouts directly to the Deity. It's not a prayer—it's man to man*) Oh, God! You know Vinnie's not a miserable sinner! She's a damn fine woman. She shouldn't be made to suffer. (VINNIE *appears on stairway in her nightgown. She is very weak*)

VINNIE. What's the matter, Clare, what's wrong?

FATHER. (*Not hearing her*) It's got to stop, I tell you, it's got to stop! Have mercy, I say!

VINNIE. (*At foot of stairs*) What's the matter, Clare?

FATHER. Have mercy, damn it!

VINNIE. (*Coming into room*) What's wrong? (FATHER *turns and sees* VINNIE *and rushes to her. They meet dead center*)

FATHER. Vinnie—Vinnie, what are you doing down here? You shouldn't be out of bed—you get right back upstairs.

VINNIE. (*Her* R. *arm around his neck*) Oh, Clare. I heard you call. Do you need me?

FATHER. (*Quietly*) Vinnie—I know now how much I need you. Get well, Vinnie. I'll be baptized. I promise. I'll be baptized.

VINNIE. (*Puts* L. *arm around his neck*) You will?

FATHER. I'll do anything.

VINNIE. Oh, Clare—

FATHER. We'll go to Europe together, just we two. You won't have to worry about the children or the household accounts. (VINNIE *starts to faint*) Vinnie! (*He picks her up in his arms*)

DR. LLOYD. Don't worry, Mr. Day—she'll be all right now. Bless you for what you have done.

FATHER. What did I do?

DR. LLOYD. You promised to be baptized.

FATHER. (*His concern over* VINNIE'S *fainting has made him forget, and he is genuinely surprised at* DR. LLOYD'S *statement*) I did? (*Suddenly he remembers and stamps his foot*) Oh, God! (*With* VINNIE *in his arms,* HE *turns and stomps towards stairs*)

QUICK CURTAIN

ACT THREE

SCENE 1

The same.
A month later. Mid-afternoon.
The clock says four-fifteen.
Bowl of fruit is not on table.
VINNIE *is on sofa, working on her petit-point.*
MARGARET *enters, as usual uncomfortable at being up-*
stairs. SHE *is trying to brush her apron, fix her hair and*
sleeves, all at once.

MARGARET. (*Coming* D.C.) You wanted to speak to me, Ma'am?
VINNIE. Yes, Margaret, about tomorrow morning's breakfast—
we must plan it very carefully.
MARGARET. (*Puzzled*) Mr. Day hasn't complained to me about
his breakfasts lately. As a matter of fact, I've been blessing my
luck!
VINNIE. Oh no, it's not that. But tomorrow morning I'd like
something for his breakfast that would surprise him.
MARGARET. (*Doubtfully*) Surprising Mr. Day is always a bit
of a risk, Ma'am. My motto with him has always been let well
enough alone.
VINNIE. But if we think of something he especially likes, Margaret; what would you say to kippers?
MARGARET. Well, I've served him kippers, but I don't recall
his ever saying he liked them.
VINNIE. He's never said he didn't like them, has he?
MARGARET. They've never got a stamp on the floor out of him
one way or the other.
VINNIE. If Mr. Day doesn't say he doesn't like a thing you can
assume that he does. Let's take a chance on kippers, Mar-
garet.
MARGARET. Very well, Ma'am. (MARGARET *starts out*)
VINNIE. (*Innocently*) And, Margaret—You'd better have
enough breakfast for two extra places.
MARGARET. (*Knowingly, comes* D.C. *again*) Oh—so that's it!

We're going to have company again?

VINNIE. Yes, my cousin Miss Cartwright and her friend are coming back from Springfield. I'm afraid they'll get here just about breakfast time.

MARGARET. Well, in that case I'd better make some of my Sunday morning hot biscuits, too.

VINNIE. Yes. We know Mr. Day likes those.

MARGARET. I've been getting him to church with them for the last fifteen years. (MARGARET *starts up* C.) (*Door off* R. *slams. She looks there*) Oh, it's Mr. Clarence, Ma'am. (MARGARET *goes off* L.) (CLARENCE *enters* R. *with a large box, wrapped*)

CLARENCE. (*To back of table*) Here it is, Mother. (*After he puts box on table, he puts his hat on side table* U.R.C.)

VINNIE. (*Rises. Crosses to back of table—puts her petit-point on side table* U.R.C.) Oh, it was still in the store! They hadn't sold it! I'm so relieved. Didn't you admire it, Clarence?

CLARENCE. (*On* VINNIE'S R. *Hedging*) Well, it is unusual.

VINNIE. (*Unwrapping package*) You know I saw this down there the day before I got sick. I was walking through the bric-a-brac section and it caught my eye. I was so tempted to buy it. And all the time I lay ill I just couldn't get it out of my head. I can't understand how it could stay in the store all this time without somebody snatching it up? (*She takes it out of package. It is a large china pug-dog*) (CLARENCE *moves empty box to* R. *of table. He has taken lid of box as* VINNIE *takes it off and puts* D.R. *on table*) There! Isn't that the darlingest thing you ever saw! It does need a ribbon, though. I've got the very thing somewhere. Oh, yes, I know. (*She leaves dog on table and goes to side table* L., *gets ribbon out of drawer, singing "Sweet Marie" softly as she goes*)

CLARENCE. Isn't John home yet?

VINNIE. I haven't seen him—why?

CLARENCE. Well, you know we've been working, and John went down to collect our money.

VINNIE. (*Crossing to back of table* R. *again, ties ribbon on dog*) That's fine. Oh, Clarence, I have a secret for just the two of us! Who do you think is coming to visit us tomorrow?—Cousin Cora and Mary!

CLARENCE. Yes, I know.

VINNIE. How did you know?

84

CLARENCE. I happened to get a letter. (*Front door slams*) (*Enter* JOHN *carrying two pockages of medicine* C. *from* R.)

VINNIE. (*Holding up dog*) John, did you ever see anything so sweet?

JOHN. (*At* U.L. *of* C.) What *is* it?

VINNIE. It's a pug-dog. Your father would never let me have a real one, but he can't object to one made of china. This ribbon needs pressing. I'll take it down and have Margaret do it right away. (VINNIE *exits to* L., *taking dog with her*)

CLARENCE. What did you bring home more medicine for? (*Then with sudden fright, moves toward* JOHN) Dr. Bartlett paid us off, didn't he?

JOHN. Yes.

CLARENCE. You had me worried for a minute. (*Heaving a great sigh of relief—then happily moves* D.C. *then* D.R.) When I went down to McCreery's to get the pug-dog for Mother, I ordered the daisiest suit you ever saw. Dr. Bartlett owed us sixteen dollars apiece, and the suit was only fifteen. Isn't that lucky? Come on, give me my money. (*Crosses back to* JOHN)

JOHN. (*Has moved* D.C. *when* CLARENCE *mentioned suit. Very diffidently*) Clarence, Dr. Bartlett paid us off in medicine.

CLARENCE. (*Aghast*) (R. *of* C.) You let him pay us off with that old Beneficent Balm?

JOHN. (*Proudly*) Well, he thanked us, too,—"for our services to mankind."

CLARENCE. (*In agony*) What about me? I belong to mankind. What about my suit?

JOHN. (*Sympathetically—crosses, puts packages on bench*) You'll just have to wait for your suit.

CLARENCE. I can't wait! I've got to have it tomorrow—and besides, they're making the alterations. I've got to pay for it this afternoon. (*Moves to* L.C.) Fifteen dollars!

JOHN. (*Helpfully*) Offer them fifteen bottles of medicine. (CLARENCE *gives it a little desperate thought*)

CLARENCE. They wouldn't take it. McCreery's don't sell medicine. (*He moves towards mantel, then up and down* L.)

JOHN. That's too bad. (JOHN *crosses to window and looks out*) Here comes Father.

CLARENCE. I'll have to brace Father for that fifteen dollars.

85

I hate to do it, but I've got to—that's all—I've got to! (*Crosses to* R.C. *as if to window, but stops when door slams*)

JOHN. (*Picking up packages*) I'm not going to be here when you do. (*Door slams*) I'd better hide this somewhere, anyway. (*He starts up* R. *back of table to* R. *of arch*) (FATHER *enters and looks into room, before* JOHN *can get out, so he hides packages behind him.* FATHER *has his newspaper with him*)

CLARENCE. (*At right of table*) Good afternoon, sir.

FATHER. How's your Mother, Clarence? Where is she?

CLARENCE. She's all right. She's downstairs with Margaret. Oh, Father . . . (FATHER *exits* L. *and we hear him calling downstairs*) (JOHN *rushes upstairs—hiding packages as best he can*)

FATHER. (*Off-stage*) Vinnie! I'm home. (FATHER *reappears in arch, minus hat and stick, carrying newspaper*)

CLARENCE. Father, Mother will be well enough to go to church with us next Sunday.

FATHER. (*Coming* D.R. *of* C.) That's fine, Clarence. That's fine. (*He starts toward his chair* D.R.)

CLARENCE. (*Stepping in front of* FATHER) Father, have you noticed that I haven't been kneeling down in church lately?

FATHER. (*Good-naturedly*) Don't let your Mother catch you at it.

CLARENCE. (*Very abruptly*) Then I've got to have a new suit of clothes.

FATHER. (*After a puzzled look*) Clarence, you're not even making sense!

CLARENCE. But a fellow doesn't feel right in cut-down clothes —especially your clothes. That's why I can't kneel down in church—I can't do anything in them you wouldn't do.

FATHER. Well, that's a damn good thing. If my old clothes make you behave yourself I don't think you should ever wear anything else.

CLARENCE. (*Desperately*) Oh, no! You're you—and I'm me! I want to be myself! Besides, you're older and there are things I've got to do that I wouldn't do at your age.

FATHER. Clarence, you should never do anything I wouldn't do.

CLARENCE. Oh—yes, look, for instance. Suppose I should want to kneel down in front of a girl?

FATHER. Why in heaven's name should you want to do a thing

like that?

CLARENCE. Well, I've got to get married some time. I've got to propose to a girl *sometime.*

FATHER. *(Exasperated)* Before you're married, I hope, you'll be earning your own clothes. Don't get the idea into your head I'm going to support you and a wife, too. Besides, at your age, Clarence—

CLARENCE. *(Hastily—Desperately)* Oh, I'm not going to be married right away, but for fifteen dollars I can get a good suit of clothes. (VINNIE *enters* C. *from* L.)

FATHER. *(Bewildered and irritated, loudly)* Clarence! You're beginning to talk as crazy as your Mother. (VINNIE *comes right down to* FATHER'S *side, putting her hand on his shoulder—paying no attention to his last remark—Kindly)* Oh, hello, Vinnie. *(He kisses her)* How're you feeling?

VINNIE. I'm fine, Clare! You don't have to hurry home from the office every day like this. (CLARENCE *throws himself in chair by window, sick with disappointment)* *(He pays no attention to following scene)*

FATHER. *(Crossing to sofa)* Business the way it is, no use going to the office at all.

VINNIE. But you haven't been to your club for weeks.

FATHER. *(Sits and takes out his glasses)* Can't stand the damn place. You do look better, Vinnie. What did you do today?

VINNIE. *(Moves to back of sofa)* I took a long walk and dropped in to call on Mrs. Whitehead.

FATHER. *(Opens paper and starts to read)* Well, that's fine.

VINNIE. *(Suddenly excited)* It was the most fortunate thing that ever happened. I've got wonderful news for you! Who do you think was there? Mr. Morley!

FATHER. *(Not placing him)* Morley?

VINNIE. You remember—that nice young minister who substituted for Dr. Lloyd one Sunday?

FATHER. *(Looking up from paper)* Oh, yes—bright young fellow, preached a good sensible sermon.

VINNIE. It was the only time I ever saw you put five dollars in the plate!

FATHER. Ought to be more ministers like him. I could get along with that young man without any trouble at all. *(He goes back to his paper)*

87

VINNIE. Well, Clare, his parish is in Audubon—you know, way up above Harlem.

FATHER. (*Reading paper*) Is that so?

VINNIE. Isn't that wonderful? Nobody knows you up there. You'll be perfectly safe!

FATHER. (*Repeats without thinking*) Safe? (*Suddenly getting the thought*) Vinnie, what the devil are you talking about?

VINNIE. I've been all over everything with Mr. Morley and he's agreed to baptize you.

FATHER. (*Good naturedly*) Oh, he has—the young whipper-snapper! Damn nice of him! (*Goes back to his paper*)

VINNIE. (*Moving a little to* L.) We can go up there any morning, Clare—we don't even have to make an appointment.

FATHER. (*His attention still on paper*) Vinnie, you're making a lot of plans for nothing. Who said I was going to be baptized at all?

VINNIE (*Aghast*) Why, Clare! You did!

FATHER. (*Looking up*) Now, Vinnie!—

VINNIE. You gave me your promise—your sacred promise. (*Crossing to* c. *to point out spot and then down to* R. *of sofa*) You stood right on that spot and said "I'll be baptized. I promise—I'll be baptized!"

FATHER. What if I did?

VINNIE. (*Amazed*) Aren't you a man of your word?

FATHER. (*Rises, with righteous indignation*) Vinnie, that was under entirely different circumstances. We all thought you were dying, so naturally I said that to cheer you up. As a matter of fact, the doctor told me that's what cured you. So it seems to me pretty ungrateful of you to press this matter any further.

VINNIE. You gave me your Sacred Promise!

FATHER. (*Getting annoyed*) Vinnie, you were sick when I said that. Now you're well again. (MARGARET *enters with pug-dog, which now has the freshly pressed ribbon tied around its neck. She puts it on table.* FATHER *doesn't notice her*)

MARGARET. Is that all right, Mrs. Day?

VINNIE. (*Dismissingly, keeping her attention on* FATHER) That's fine, Margaret, thank you. (MARGARET *exits*) (VINNIE *goes right on talking as though there had been no interrup-*

tion) My being well has nothing to do with it! You gave me your word! You gave the Lord your word. (FATHER *throws paper on sofa, then puts glasses away*) If you had seen how eager Mr. Morley was to bring you into the fold. (FATHER *swings around* L. *end of sofa towards* C. *arch. She follows him*) And you're going to march yourself up to his church some morning before you go to the office and be christened. (FATHER *sees pug-dog, and stops*) If you think for one minute that I'm going to . . .

FATHER. (*Is now staring at it intently*) What in the name of heaven is that?

VINNIE. (*On his* L.) If you think I'm going to let you add the sin of breaking your Solemn and Sacred Promise—

FATHER. (U.C.) I demand to know what that repulsive object is!

VINNIE. It's perfectly plain what it is—it's a pug-dog!

FATHER. What's it doing in this house?

VINNIE. (*Trying unsuccessfully to be defiant*) I wanted it and I bought it.

FATHER. You paid good money for that?

VINNIE. Clare, we're not talking about that! We're talking about you! Don't try to change the subject!

FATHER. How much did you pay for that atrocity.

VINNIE. I don't know. I sent Clarence down for it. Listen to me, Clare—

FATHER. Clarence, what did you pay for that?

CLARENCE. (*Rises*) I didn't pay anything. I charged it.

FATHER. (*Looking at* VINNIE) Charged it! I might have known. (*To* CLARENCE) How much was it?

CLARENCE. Fifteen dollars.

FATHER. Fifteen dollars for that eyesore?

VINNIE. (*Crossing to back of table* R. *taking dog in her arms*) Don't you call that lovely work of art an eyesore! (FATHER *moves* D.C.) That will look beautiful sitting on a red cushion by the fireplace in the parlor. (*She puts dog down on table*)

FATHER. (C.) If that sits in the parlor, I won't! Furthermore, I don't even want it in the same house with me. Get it out of here! (*He starts for arch*)

VINNIE. (*Crossing up and stopping him*) You're just using that for an excuse. You're not going to get out of this room until you set a date for your baptism.

FATHER. (*Starts to stairs—speaking as he is going up*) Well, I'll tell you one thing: I'll never be baptized as long as that hideous monstrosity is in this house. (HE *stomps upstairs and off*)

VINNIE. (*Calling after him*) All right! (SHE *goes to pug-dog back of table.* SHE *makes up her mind*) All right! It goes back this afternoon and he's christened first thing in the morning. (*Puts dog in box*)

CLARENCE. But, Mother—

VINNIE. Clarence, you heard your father say that he'd be baptized as soon as I got this pug-dog out of the house. (*Takes ribbon from dog*) You hurry right back to McCreery's with it—and be sure they credit us with fifteen dollars. (*The "fifteen dollars" rings a bell in* CLARENCE'S *mind*)

CLARENCE. (*To* R. *of table*) Oh, Mother, while I was at Mc-Creery's I happened to see a suit I liked very much and the suit was only fifteen dollars.

VINNIE. (*Regretfully*) Well, Clarence, I'm afraid your suit will have to wait until after I get your father christened.

CLARENCE. (*Hopefully*) No. I meant that since the suit cost just the same as the pug-dog, if I exchanged the pug-dog for the suit—

VINNIE. Why, yes, then your suit wouldn't cost Father anything! . . . That's very bright of you, Clarence, to think of that!

CLARENCE. (*Crossing to back of table*) I'd better start right away before McCreery's closes. (*He picks up box cover*)

VINNIE. Yes. Let's see. If we're going to take your Father all the way up to Audubon—Clarence, you stop at Ryerson and Brown's on your way back and tell them to have a cab here at eight o'clock tomorrow morning.

CLARENCE. Mother, a cab! Do you think you ought to?

VINNIE. Well, we can't walk to Audubon.

CLARENCE. (*Warningly*) But you know what a cab does to Father.

VINNIE. This is an important occasion.

CLARENCE. (*With a shrug*) All right. A Brougham or a Victoria?

VINNIE. Get one of their best cabs—the kind they use at funerals.

90

CLARENCE. Mother! Those cost two dollars an hour! And if Father gets mad—

VINNIE. If your Father starts to argue in the morning, you remember—

CLARENCE. Oh, he agreed to it! We both heard him!

VINNIE. (*Regretfully*) I did have my heart set on this. (*An idea comes to her*) Still—if they didn't sell him in all that time— (*She gives dog a reassuring pat. Then rolls string and ribbon around her finger. She begins to sing "Sweet Marie" happily*) (FATHER *comes down the stairs*) (CLARENCE *puts lid on box, then takes his hat and box and goes happily and quickly out*) (FATHER *is startled at* CLARENCE *rushing by him*) (*We hear door slam*) I hope you notice that Clarence is returning the pug-dog?

FATHER. That's a sign you're getting your faculties back. (FATHER *starts toward sofa, but stops* C.) (VINNIE *is still singing quietly to herself in a satisfied way. She puts ribbon and string on side table* U.R.C.) Good to hear you singing again, Vinnie. (*Suddenly remembering*) Oh!—on my way uptown I stopped in at Tiffany's and bought you a little something. Thought you might like it. (*He takes out of his pocket a small ring-box and holds it out to her. She runs to take it as soon as he says Tiffany's*) (FATHER *goes to sofa—takes up paper and sits*)

VINNIE. (*She opens it eagerly*) Oh, Clare. What a lovely ring! (*She takes ring out and examines it. Then puts it on her finger and admires it*)

FATHER. I'm glad if it pleases you, Lavinia.

VINNIE. Oh, Clare. (*Crosses back of sofa, putting ring-box on table as she passes. Kisses him*) I don't know how to thank you.

FATHER. It's thanks enough for me to have you up and around again. (VINNIE *moves to* D.C. *admiring ring*) When you take to your bed this house is like a tomb. There's no excitement! (*He snaps open his paper*)

VINNIE. Clare, this is the loveliest ring you ever bought me. (*Crosses and sits beside him*) Now that I have this, you needn't buy me any more rings.

FATHER. (*Rather pleased. He starts to straighten ribbon of his glasses*) Well, if you don't want any more.

91

VINNIE. (*Still looking at ring*) What I'd really like now is a nice diamond necklace.

FATHER. (*Aghast*) Vinnie, do you know how much a diamond necklace costs?

VINNIE. I know, Clare, but don't you see—your getting me this ring shows that I mean a little something to you. Now a diamond necklace—

FATHER. Good God,—if you don't know how I feel about you by this time—(*He looks away*) We've been married for twenty years and I've loved you every minute of it.

VINNIE. (*Hardly believing her ears*) What did you say, Clare?

FATHER. (*Turning to her sharply*) I said we've been married twenty years and I've loved you every minute. (*He looks away*) (VINNIE's *eyes fill with tears, at* FATHER's *definite statement of his love*) But if I have to buy out jewelry stores to prove it—if I haven't shown it in my words and actions I might as well—(*He turns back and sees* VINNIE *crying—speaks with resigned helplessness*) What have I done now?

VINNIE. It's all right, Clare—I'm just so happy.

FATHER. Happy?

VINNIE. You said you loved me—and this beautiful ring—that's something else I never expected. (*She puts her arm through his and cuddles her head on his shoulder*) (FATHER *is pleased*) Oh, Clare, I love surprises.

FATHER. (*Seriously*) That's another thing I have never understood about you, Vinnie. Now I like to know what to expect. Then I'm prepared to meet it.

VINNIE. (*Her head on his shoulder*) Yes, I know. But, Clare, life would be pretty dull if we always knew what was coming.

FATHER. Well, it's certainly not dull around here,—in this house you never know what's going to hit you tomorrow. (*He laughs heartily at his own joke*)

VINNIE. (*To herself*) Tomorrow! (*She starts to sing, "Sweet Marie," softly,* FATHER *listening to her happily*) "Every daisy in the dell, Knows my *secret,* knows it well, And yet I dare not *tell* (*She turns her eyes up towards him*) Sweet Marie!

CURTAIN

(*Start Curtain down very slowly at the word "Secret"—at the beginning of the word "Sweet"—start down very fast*)

ACT THREE

Scene Two

The same.
The next morning. Breakfast.
The clock says eight-thirty.
The bowl which had fruit in it now has flowers in it.
VINNIE'S *prayer-book is now on side table* U.R.C.
The fruit is at VINNIE'S *place.* FATHER *and the two elder*
BOYS *are eating kippers. The young* BOYS *have their por-*
ridge as usual.
The WHOLE FAMILY *except* JOHN *and* VINNIE *is at table*
eating quietly but in good spirits.
The BOYS *are dressed in their Sunday clothes.* CLARENCE
is still in black suit.
MAGGIE, *the new maid, is at side table* R.C.—*back to audi-*
ence, with a plate of hot biscuits on a tray.
There are two letters R. *of* FATHER'S *place.*

JOHN. (*Entering from upstairs*) Mother says she'll be right
down. (*He sits at table*) (MAGGIE *comes down to serve* FATHER,
leaving tray on side table. As FATHER *takes a biscuit, he*
glances up at her and shows some little surprise)

FATHER. Who are you? What's your name?

MAGGIE. Margaret, sir.

FATHER. Can't be Margaret. We've got one Margaret in the
house.

MAGGIE. At home they call me Maggie, sir.

FATHER. All right, Maggie. (MAGGIE *continues serving bis-*
cuits to CLARENCE *and* JOHN, *then leaves them on table to* L.
of JOHN—*then crosses* U.L.C. *and waits*) Boys, if her name's
Margaret, that's a good sign. Maybe she'll stay awhile. You
know, your mother used to be just the same about cooks as
she is about maids. Never could keep them, for some reason.
Well, one day about fifteen years ago—yes, it was right after
you were born, John—my, you were a homely baby. (THEY
all laugh, at JOHN's *expense*) I came home that night all tired
out and what did I find?—no dinner because the cook had
left. Well, I decided I'd had just about enough of that, so I
marched over to the employment agency myself, and said to
the woman in charge, "Where do you keep the cooks?" She

93

tried to hold me up with a lot of red tape folderol but I just walked into the room where the girls were waiting, looked 'em over, saw Margaret, pointed at her and said "I'll take that one." I walked her home with me, she cooked dinner that night and she's been cooking for us ever since. (*He takes a bite of fish*) Damn good cook, too. (*He stamps on floor three times*)

VINNIE. (*Enters down stairs—dressed in a very handsome white dress*) Good morning Clare—(*She crosses to chair D.L. and puts her bonnet on it. Then crosses and sits at table. She is a little self-conscious of her dress because of the occasion*) Good morning, boys. (*All BOYS rise—and say "Good morning"*) (*FATHER rises—crosses above table to VINNIE'S chair, drawing it out for her. He notices that she is very dressed up*)

FATHER. Good morning, Vinnie. (*After she sits, HE starts above table to his chair, noticing boy's clothes as he passes*) Sit down, boys. (*He stands by his chair for just a moment, speaking happily*) Everybody's all dressed up.—What's on the program? (*He sits*)

VINNIE. (*Dodging the real issue*) This afternoon May Lewis's mother is giving a party for all the children in May's dancing class. Harlan's going to that.

HARLAN. I don't want to go, Mother.

VINNIE. Why, Harlan, don't you want to go to a party and get ice cream and cake?

HARLAN. May Lewis always tries to kiss me. (*This is greeted with family laughter*)

FATHER. (*Genially*) When you're a little older, Harlan, you won't object to girls wanting to kiss you. (*He laughs—then suddenly*)—Will he, Clarence? (*They all laugh at CLARENCE who blushes*) (*MARGARET comes hurrying C. from L. She is a little anxious*)

MARGARET. What's wanting? (*She goes between JOHN and VIN-NIE*)

FATHER. Margaret, these kippers are *good*. (*MARGARET makes her usual deprecatory gesture*) Haven't had kippers for a long time. I'm glad you remembered I like them.

MARGARET. Yes, sir. (*MARGARET and VINNIE exchange knowing looks. MARGARET goes out happy, C. to L.*)

FATHER. What got into Margaret this morning? Hot biscuits,

94

too!

VINNIE. She knows how fond you are of them. (*There is a second's pause, then doorbell rings*) (MAGGIE *goes to answer it*) (*Nervously*) Well, who can that be? It can't be the postman, because he's been here.

FATHER. (*With sly humor*) Clarence has been getting a good many special deliveries lately. Is that business deal going through, Clarence? (FAMILY *has a laugh at* CLARENCE *again*) (MAGGIE *comes back into room with a suit-box*)

MAGGIE. This is for you, Mr. Day. Where shall I put it?

CLARENCE. (*Hastily*) Oh, that's for me, I think. Take it upstairs, please, Maggie. (SHE *starts to do so*)

FATHER. (*Getting· out his glasses*) Wait a minute, Maggie, bring it here. Let's see it. (MAGGIE *brings it down to table, toward* FATHER) (CLARENCE *rises as she gets near him, and takes box from her*) (MAGGIE *exits* C. *to* L.)

CLARENCE. (*Just showing it, but trying to get it away*) See, it's for me, Father—Clarence Day, Jr. (*He hurries up to* C. *arch, but stops short as Father speaks*)

FATHER. Let me look! (CLARENCE *does so, slowly. He fears an explosion*) It's from McCreery's and it's marked charge. What is it? (CLARENCE *looks to Mother*)

VINNIE. It's all right, Clare. It's nothing for you to worry about.

FATHER. Well, at least I think I should know what's being charged to me. What is it?

VINNIE. Now, Clare, stop your fussing. It's a new suit of clothes for Clarence. It isn't costing you a penny.

FATHER. It's marked "Charge $15"—It's costing me fifteen dollars. And I told Clarence . . .

VINNIE. Clare, can't you take my word? It isn't costing you a penny.

FATHER. (*Taking off glasses*) I'd like to have you explain why it isn't?

VINNIE. (*Triumphantly*) Because Clarence took the pug-dog back and got the suit instead.

FATHER. Yes, and they'll charge me fifteen dollars for the suit.

VINNIE. Nonsense, Clare, we gave them the pug-dog for the suit. Don't you see?

FATHER. Then they'll charge me fifteen dollars for the pug-dog.

VINNIE. But, Clare, they can't—We haven't got the pug-dog.

FATHER. (*She has him winging for a second*) Just a minute, Vinnie, there's something wrong with your reasoning. (*He slaps his napkin on table, swings his chair so he faces front, while he tries to figure it out*)

VINNIE. (*Laughs lightly*) I'm surprised at you, Clare, and you're supposed to be so good at figures. (FATHER *looks at* VINNIE *resentfully*) Why, it's perfectly clear to me.

FATHER. (*Emphatically*) My dear Vinnie, they'll charge me for one thing or the other.

VINNIE. (*Firmly*) Don't you let them!

FATHER. (FATHER *gets up and crosses to* L.C.—*staring at* VINNIE —*then he walks over to window, in his irritation saying*) Well, McCreery's aren't giving away suits and they aren't giving away pug-dogs. Can't you get it through your—? (*Looking out window*) Oh! Oh! Oh, God!

VINNIE. What is it, Clare? What's wrong?

FATHER. (*Backs away to near his chair at table*) Don't anyone answer the door.

VINNIE. Who is it? Who's coming?

FATHER. Those damn women are back!

JOHN. What women?

FATHER. Cora and that little idiot. (CLARENCE *dashes madly up stairs, clutching box with his new suit*) (VINNIE *rises— moves up towards arch*) They're moving in on us again, bag and baggage. (*Doorbell rings*) Don't let them in! (JOHN *puts napkin in ring*)

VINNIE. (*Comes down to back of her chair*) Clarence Day, as if we could turn our own relatives away! (*She goes up to* L. *of arch*)

FATHER. Tell them to get back in that cab and drive right on to Ohio. If they're extravagant enough to take cabs when horse-cars go right by our door—(MAGGIE *crosses hall to answer bell*)

VINNIE. (*Coming down to her chair again*) Now, Clare—you be quiet and behave yourself. They're here and there's nothing you can do about it. (*She starts toward hall—at* L. *side of arch*)

FATHER. (*Shouting*) Why do they always pounce on us with-

96

out warning—the damn gypsies! (*He moves* D.R.)

VINNIE. (*From arch, loudly to* CLARE) Shh! Shh!—(*Immediately following this, in her best welcoming tone and with arms extended*) Cora! (JOHN, HARLAN *and* WHITNEY *rise*)

CORA. (*Entering—kisses* VINNIE) How are you, Vinnie. (*As she moves* D.R.) We've been so worried about you. (CORA *greets* HARLAN *and* WHITNEY *as she passes below table. They answer her*) (MARY *enters, kisses* VINNIE. *They come into room.* VINNIE *to* U.R. *of* C.) (MARY *to* U.L. *of* C. *She looks around room for* CLARENCE) Harlan—and Whitney! (MAGGIE *follows in and stands* U.L. *of arch and waits for orders*) And Cousin Clare. (CORA *kisses* FATHER *on cheek*) Here we are again! (FATHER *gives her a quick frosty smile*) (WHITNEY *and* HARLAN *sit—and put napkin in ring*) (CORA *crosses to* R. *upper corner of table*) And John!

JOHN. Hello, Cousin Cora.

CORA. Where is Clarence?

MARY. Yes, where is Clarence?

VINNIE. John, go tell Clarence that Cousin Cora and *Mary* are here.

JOHN. (*Exits upstairs*) Yes, Mother.

VINNIE. You got here just in time to have breakfast with us.

CORA. We had breakfast at the depot.

VINNIE. Well, as a matter of fact, we'd just finished.

FATHER. (*With cold dignity*) *I* haven't finished my breakfast!

VINNIE. Well, then sit down, Clare. (FATHER *returns to his chair slowly, in stony silence*) (*To* CORA *and* MARY) Margaret gave us kippers this morning and Clare's so fond of kippers . . . Why don't we all sit down? (VINNIE *indicates empty places and* GIRLS *sit*) (CORA *in* JOHN's *chair*) (MARY *in* CLARENCE's) Maggie, clear those things away. (*She indicates dishes in front of girls*) (MAGGIE *does so, puts dishes on tray* U.R.C. *then exits with them* C. *to* L.) (FATHER *puts on glasses, opens letter and starts to read it*) Clare, don't let your kippers get cold. (VINNIE *sits* L. *of table, moving her chair up so it is almost on level with* CORA's. *There is a second's uncomfortable pause*) Now—tell us all about Springfield. (JOHN *comes downstairs, and exits* R.)

CORA. We had a wonderful month—but tell us about you, Cousin Vinnie. You must have had a terrible time.

97

VINNIE. Yes, I was pretty sick, but I'm all right again now.

CORA. What was it?

VINNIE. Well, the doctors don't know exactly, but they did say this, whatever it was they've never seen anything like it before.

CORA. You certainly look well enough now. Doesn't she, Cousin Clare?

FATHER. (*Angered by letter*) Oh, God! (JOHN *starts upstairs with bags*)

VINNIE. What's the matter, Clare? What's wrong?

FATHER. (*Seeing* JOHN *on stairs*) John! John! (JOHN *is halfway up stairs with bags. He comes running down, leaves bags in hall and goes to* R. *of* FATHER)

JOHN. Yes, Father?

FATHER. (*Quietly, looking at letter*) Have you been going around this town selling medicine?

JOHN. (*A little frightened*) Yes, Father.

FATHER. Dog medicine?

JOHN. No, Father, not dog medicine.

FATHER. (*Looking at* JOHN) It must have been dog medicine.

JOHN. It wasn't dog medicine, Father—

FATHER. (*Indicating letter he has been reading*) Mrs. Sprague writes me that you sold her a bottle of this medicine and her little boy gave some of it to their dog and it killed him! Now she wants ten dollars for a new dog.

JOHN. He shouldn't have given it to a dog. It's for humans— (FATHER *looks at* JOHN) Why, it was Bartlett's Beneficent Balm—made from a secret formula.

FATHER. Have you been going around to our friends and neighbors selling them some damned Dr. Munyon patent nostrum?

JOHN. It's good medicine, Father.—I can prove it by Mother.

FATHER. (*Quietly*) Vinnie, what do you know about this?

VINNIE. Nothing, Clare; but I'm sure that John . . .

JOHN. No. I mean that day Mother—

FATHER. (*Firmly*) That's enough. You're going to every house where you sold a bottle of that concoction and buy it all back.

JOHN. (*Dismayed*) But it's a dollar a bottle.

FATHER. (*Putting letter in envelope*) I don't care how much it costs. I'll give you the money. How many bottles did you sell?

JOHN. (*Almost afraid to tell*) A hundred and twenty-eight.

FATHER. (*Roaring*) A hundred and twenty-eight!

VINNIE. Clare, I always told you John would make a good business man.

FATHER. (*Looks at* VINNIE *for a second. Calmly*) Well, John, I'll give you the money to buy it all back. A hundred and twenty-eight dollars. And ten more for Mrs. Sprague. (*Throws letter on table*) That's a hundred and thirty-eight dollars. (*Getting louder*) But it's coming out of your allowance. That means you'll not get another penny until that hundred and thirty-eight dollars is all paid up. (FATHER *picks up newspaper angrily and sits quietly—nothing must be done to take audience's attention from* JOHN) (JOHN *starts toward hall, counting on his fingers; when he is in back of table, he turns and addresses his* FATHER *in dismay.* JOHN's *allowance is about $25 a year*)

JOHN. I'll be twenty-one years old. (FATHER *ignores him, so* JOHN *turns and goes on up stairs with bags*)

VINNIE. (*Quietly*) Clare, you know you've always encouraged the boys to earn their own money.

FATHER. I'll handle this, Vinnie. (*He buries himself in his newspaper, so that his face is not seen by audience*) (*There is a pause*)

CORA. (*Breaking through the constraint*) Of course, Aunt Judith sent her love to all of you—

VINNIE. I haven't seen Judith for years. You'd think living so close to Springfield—maybe I could run up there before the summer's over?

CORA. She'll be leaving for Pleasantville any day now, Grandpa Ebbetts has been failing very fast and that's why I have to hurry back.

VINNIE. Hurry back? Well, you and Mary can stay with us a few days, at least?

CORA. No, Cousin Vinnie, I hate to break the news to you, but we can't even stay overnight. We're leaving on the five o'clock train this afternoon.

VINNIE. (*Disappointedly*) Oh! What a pity! (FATHER *lowers paper and takes off glasses*)

FATHER. (*Heartily*) Cora, it certainly is good to see you again.

(*To* MARY) Young lady, I think you've been enjoying your-self—you look prettier than ever. (MARY *laughs and blushes*)
WHITNEY. I'll bet Clarence will think so. (FATHER *laughs and starts eating again*) (*Doorbell rings*)
FATHER. That can't be another special delivery for Clarence! (MAGGIE *crosses hall from* L. *to* R. FATHER *to* MARY) Seems to me, while you were in Springfield our postman's been kept pretty busy. Sure you girls won't have any breakfast?
MARY. (*Rises—goes to* R. *of arch, looking up stairs for* CLAR-ENCE) No, thank you.
CORA. Oh no, thank you, Clare, we had our breakfast.
FATHER. At least you ought to have a cup of coffee with us. Vinnie, why didn't you think to order some coffee for the girls. (MAGGIE *appears again and goes to* L. *of* VINNIE)
CORA. No, no! Thank you, Cousin Clare. (VINNIE *is very self-conscious, knowing that the moment has arrived*)
MAGGIE. It's the cab, ma'am. (MAGGIE *exits* C. *to* L.)
FATHER. (*Still eating*) The cab? What cab?
VINNIE. The cab that's to take us to Audubon.
FATHER. Who's going to Audubon? (*Picks up his coffee cup and takes a sip*)
VINNIE. We all are. Cora, the most wonderful thing has happened.
CORA. What, Cousin Vinnie?
VINNIE. (*Happily*) Clare's going to be baptized this morning.
FATHER. (*He was just about to take another drink of coffee— Not believing his ears*) Vinnie—what—what are you saying?
VINNIE. (*With gentle determination*) I'm saying you're going to be baptized this morning!
FATHER. (*Putting down cup*) I am not going to be baptized this morning, or any other morning!
VINNIE. (*Getting a little excited*) You promised yesterday that as soon as I sent that pug-dog back you'd be baptized.
FATHER. (*Also getting excited*) I promised no such thing!
VINNIE. You certainly did!
FATHER. I never said anything remotely like that!
VINNIE. Clarence was right here and heard it! You ask him!
FATHER. Clarence be damned! I know what I said! I don't remember exactly, but it wasn't that!
VINNIE. Well, I remember! That's why I ordered the cab!

100

FATHER. The cab? (*Suddenly remembering*) Oh, my God, that cab! (*Rises—looks out window, then moves below* R. *corner of table*) Vinnie, you send that right back.

VINNIE. (*Rises*) I'll do no such thing. I'm going to see that you go to Heaven!

FATHER. I can't go to Heaven in a cab!

VINNIE. (*After laugh starts, she moves to* L. *of* C.) Well, you can start in a cab. I'm not sure whether they'll ever let you in Heaven, but I know they won't unless you're baptized.

FATHER. (*With dignity*) They can't keep me out of Heaven on a technicality.

VINNIE. Clare, stop quibbling! You might just as well face it—you've got to make your peace with God.

FATHER. (*Excitedly*) Until you stirred Him up, I had no trouble with God. (*He crosses* U.R.—*then down* R.C. *again*) (CORA *has been following argument with lively interest*) (MARY *has been paying no attention—now she moves towards foot of stairs—then starts towards* VINNIE)

MARY. (*Coming* D.C.) Mrs. Day? (VINNIE *answers her quickly, as if expecting* MARY *to supply her with an added argument*) (FATHER *also is interested in what she may say*)

VINNIE. Yes, Mary?

MARY. (D.C.) Where do you suppose *Clarence* is?

FATHER. (*Crossing to her*) You keep out of this, young lady! If it hadn't been for you, no one would have known whether I was baptized or not. (MARY *breaks into a loud burst of tears—runs to* R. *of arch*) Damn! Damnation! (FATHER *moves a little* U.L. *of* C.)

VINNIE. (*Crossing to them, quickly*) Harlan, Whitney, get your Sunday hats. (*Crossing* U.C. *Calls upstairs*) John! Clarence! (*She runs back of sofa to chair* D.L. *for her bonnet*) (HARLAN *and* WHITNEY *rise and push their chairs under table, then start out,* WHITNEY *around* R. *of table,* HARLAN *around* L. *of table*) (THEY *stop as* FATHER *speaks.* WHITNEY *at* R.C. *corner of table,* HARLAN *almost in front of* FATHER)

FATHER. (*With hurt dignity*) Vinnie, are you mad? Was it your plan that my own children should witness this indignity?

VINNIE. (*Picking up her bonnet*) Why, Clare, they'll be proud of you!

FATHER. (*Pointing at* HARLAN. *Exploding*) I suppose Harlan is

to be my godfather! (*With determination, he crosses to* VINNIE
D.L.) Vinnie, it's no use. (WHITNEY *and* HARLAN *move slowly
up to* L. *of arch*) (JOHN *starts down stairs, slowly*) I can't go
through with this thing, and I won't. That's final.

VINNIE. All right, Clare dear, if you feel that way about it—

FATHER. (*Turning away*) I do!

VINNIE. We won't take the children with us. (FATHER *turns
back to* VINNIE) (JOHN *enters room*) (WHITNEY *moves up to
arch after* JOHN *enters*) (HARLAN *to back of* L. *end of sofa*)

JOHN. (*Coming down* C.) Yes, Mother?

FATHER. (*Dodging an argument*) Oh, John! Vinnie, I haven't
time for anything like that this morning. I've got to take
John down to the office and give him the money to buy back
that medicine. (*To* JOHN) When I think of you going around
this town selling dog medicine—(WHITNEY *goes to* R. *of table
near sofa*)

JOHN. (*Insistently*) It wasn't dog medicine, Father.

FATHER. That's enough. We're starting downtown this minute!

VINNIE. You're doing no such thing! (FATHER *turns to* VINNIE)
You gave me your Sacred Promise that day I almost died . . .

JOHN. (*Proudly,—a chance to justify himself*) Yes, and she
would have died if we hadn't given her some of that medicine.
That proves it's good medicine. (MARY *has stopped crying and
becomes interested*)

FATHER. (*Turning slowly to* JOHN. *Aghast*) You gave your
mother some of that dog medicine!

VINNIE. Oh, no, John, you didn't!

JOHN. (*He sees something is wrong*) Yes we did, Mother. We
put some in your tea that morning. (VINNIE *sits* D.L., *a little
stunned*) (CORA *rises*)

FATHER. You did what? Without her knowing it? (JOHN *nods*)
Do you realize you might have killed your mother? You *did*
kill Mrs. Sprague's dog. (*After a solemn pause*) John, you've
done a very serious thing. (*Moves* L.) I'll have to give considerable thought as to how I'm going to punish you for this.

VINNIE. But Clare, dear!

FATHER. No, Vinnie. When I think of that day—with this
house full of doctors—Why, Cora, we even sent for the minister. (*Really moved*) Vinnie, we might have lost you! (*He*

dismisses the thought) It's all right now, thank God, you're well again. (*Pats her shoulder and moves toward* JOHN) But what *I* went through that afternoon . . . the way I felt—I'll never forget it.

VINNIE. Don't talk that way, Clare. You've forgotten it already.

FATHER. (*Turning to her*) What do you mean?

VINNIE. That was the day you gave me your Sacred Promise.

FATHER. I wouldn't have promised if I hadn't thought you were dying—and you wouldn't have almost have died if John hadn't given you that dog medicine. Don't you see, the whole thing's illegal. (JOHN *goes slowly up to* L. *of arch*)

VINNIE. Suppose I had died! (HARLAN *goes behind her chair to her* L., *frowning at* FATHER *and putting arm around her*) It wouldn't make any difference to you. You don't care whether we meet in Heaven or not—(WHITNEY *goes down to her* R., *also frowning at* FATHER)—you don't care whether you ever see me and the children again. (*She almost succeeds in crying*)

FATHER. (*Distressed*) Now, Vinnie, you're not being fair to me.

VINNIE. (*Nobly resigned*) It's all right, Clare. If you don't love us enough, there's nothing we can do about it.

FATHER. (*Exasperated*) That has nothing to do with it!—I love my family as much as any man. (*Walking away in distress—going toward* R.) There's nothing within reason I wouldn't do for you and you know it! The years I've struggled and worked just to prove—(*He has reached window and sees cab. A slight pause. He turns back, and speaks in a very sympathetic tone*) Vinnie, you're not well enough to go all the way up to Audubon.

VINNIE. (*Perkily*) I'm well enough to go if we ride.

FATHER. That trip would take all morning. And those cabs cost a dollar an hour.

VINNIE. That's one of their best cabs. That costs two dollars an hour. (FATHER *stares at her a second, horrified, half turns to window—then explodes*)

FATHER. Then why aren't you ready? Get your hat on! (*He crosses* U.C.) Damn! Damnation! (FATHER *exits* C. *to* L. *for his hat and stick*) (*Doorbell rings loudly*) (VINNIE *dashes for prayer-book which is on side table* U.R.C.—*putting on her bonnet as she runs*)

WHITNEY. (*Takes* HARLAN's *hand*) Let's watch them start! (*Running up* L. *of sofa—with* HARLAN) Come on, Cousin Cora, let's watch them start. (THEY *exit* C. *to* R.)

CORA. (*Following them off*) I wouldn't miss it. (VINNIE *starts out* C.) (MARY *runs to window*)

JOHN. (L. *in arch. Contrite*) Mother—I didn't mean to almost kill you.

VINNIE. (*Going to* JOHN) Now, don't you worry ɹout what your Father said. (*Tenderly*) It's all right, dear. (*She kisses* • *him and starts to exit, then stops*) It turned out fine! (*She exits* R.) (*We hear sound of hurrying feet upstairs.* JOHN *looks upstairs then at* MARY)

JOHN. Mary! Here comes Clarence! (JOHN *exits* C. *to* R.) (MARY *hurriedly sits in* FATHER's *chair,* D.R. CLARENCE *comes rushing down steps in his new cream-colored suit. He goes into room and quickly adjusts his new clothes. Then rushes right to* MARY. *Without saying a word he kneels in front of her.* THEY *both are starry-eyed*) (FATHER, *with hat and stick, comes into arch from* L., *sees* CLARENCE *and* MARY)

FATHER. Oh, God! (CLARENCE *springs up in embarrassment*) (VINNIE *re-enters hurriedly*)

VINNIE. What's the matter? What's wrong? (FATHER *steps down and points his cane at* CLARENCE)

CLARENCE. (*Quickly*) Nothing's wrong. Mother—nothing's wrong. (*Hurriedly for want of something to say*) Going to the office, Father?

FATHER. No, I'm going to be baptized, damn it! (*He slams his hat on angrily and stalks out, crossing in front of* VINNIE) (VINNIE *gives a triumphant nod and follows him. Curtain starts down and as it falls,* CLARENCE *again kneels at* MARY's *feet*)

CURTAIN

CURTAIN CALLS

A Family Group, posed in the very stiff style of photographs of the 1880's.

Mother and Father seated on sofa. Mother right. Father left. Harlan seated on floor between them. Whitney standing just right of sofa. Clarence and John behind sofa. Clarence back of Mother, John back of Father.

SECOND CALL

Clarence seated in armchair, left of table R.C. Mary standing at his left, with her hand on his shoulder.

THIRD CALL

The four maids—with Margaret in the center. They face right, but their heads are turned over their left shoulders— smiling broadly. They stand close together, leaning forward so as to emphasize their bustles, hands clasped in front of them.

FOURTH CALL

The four Boys. Arranged according to height. Very stiff. All wearing their straw hats.

FIFTH CALL

Father and Mother.

Posed a la the 80's. They hold the pose for a moment—then break it and accept the applause as themselves.

Then they return to the 1880's pose.

SIXTH CALL

Entire Company.

Mother	Father
Lloyd	Cora
John	Clarence
Harlan	Mary
Margaret	Whitney
Nora	Delia
Maggie	Annie

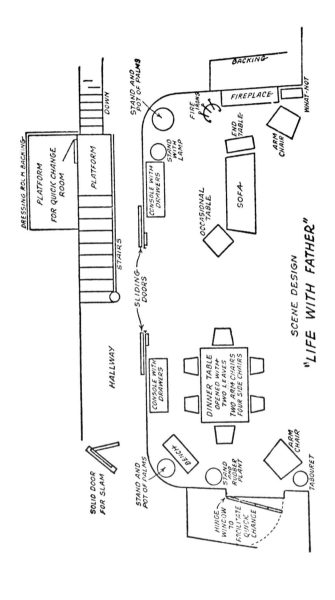

SCENE DESIGN
"LIFE WITH FATHER"

PROPERTY LIST

All furniture and props must be of the 1880's period.

ON STAGE

1 Tabourette
  1 vase of flowers
  2 books
1 silver topped glass jar (for cigars)
  Cigars
  Match stand
  Old fashioned Parlor matches
1 Arm chair
1 Stand
1 Jardiniere
1 Rubber plant
2 Stands
2 Jardinieres
2 Palms
2 Side tables or console tables, with drawers
2 Large Vases
4 Smaller vases
2 Brass framed photographs
1 Set fire irons
1 Set andirons
1 Bronze clock
2 Urns with plumes
2 Candelabras
1 What-not stand and ornaments (about 12 pieces)
1 Small armchair
1 End table
  Vase of flowers
  3 books
  1 Figurette
1 Sofa
1 Cushion
1 Occasional table
  1 Lamp
  1 Large ornament
  2 Framed photographs
1 Extension table—6' x 4'
4 Small chairs

2 Armchairs
1 Stool
Drapes for window and door in hallway
Lace curtains for window
Lambrican for mantel-piece
6 Drinking glasses—for milk
18 Service plates
12 smaller plates
12 glass plates for fruit
12 glass castors for fruit
6 cereal bowls
18 Coffee cups and saucers
12 butter pats
12 knives
12 forks
12 teaspoons
6 fruit spoons
1 Silver toast rack
4 silver salt and pepper shakers
1 serving spoon
1 serving fork
6 silver napkin rings
4 platters
1 silver coffee pot
1 silver creamer
1 silver sugar bowl
1 silver sugar spoon
3 medium sized glass plates for cakes
2 large black trays
1 large fancy tray
1 large silver tray
1 small silver tray
1 silver salver
1 small round tray
1 silver teapot
1 silver tea-set sugar bowl
12 tea cups and saucers
6 small tea spoons

4 breakfast table cloths   24 breakfast napkins
12 tea napkins

The above list of tableware includes coverage for breakage etc.

FOR OFF STAGE USE

2 large silencers for breakfast table
1 False table-top
Copy of New York Times—1888
Copy of New York Evening Sun—1888
Copy of Youth's Companion—1888
1 Old fashioned doorbell on springs
1 Postman's whistle
1 Stereoscope
Several pictures for same
Supply of writing paper and envelopes
     Blue—Pink—Lavender—White
     White business envelopes—
     Pencils
Stage money
3 coins—half dollar
1 handsome leather wallet—for Father
1 coin purse—for Father
Crash effect of ANNIE falling downstairs
     tin tray
     Broken dishes and boxes
     1 padded stick—for falling body
Brown wrapping paper (for medicine boxes)
Blue wrapping paper (for pug-dog and suitboxes)
Ball of white string
Ball of heavy twine
1 box of Tiddlewinks
1 Sheet music "The Merry Farmer"
1 Piano—Offstage
24 household bills of different sizes and colors
1 handsome household account book
Newspaper clipping—for JOHN

2 shoe boxes—to be wrapped for BOX LUNCH
Supply of boxes for medicine—each supposed to hold 2 dozen 8 ounce bottles
2 eight ounce old fashioned medicine bottles
Labels for same—as per SCRIPT
1 Copper tea kettle
2 hand towels
1 Doctor's satchel
1 China pug dog
Box for china dog
Supply of tissue paper
3 yards of red ribbon—1½ inch wide—Cut in two pieces—one piece mussed, one piece ironed
1 Jewelers' ring box
1 ring—must be very handsome
1 suit box
Label for same
1 Purse—For VINNIE
1 Fancy table cloth
2 Ladies traveling bags—of 1880
1 Handsome white prayer book—for VINNIE
1 Small black prayer book for Dr. Lloyd
2 Canes—for FATHER
1 Watch and chain, cigar cutter for FATHER
Eye-glasses and ribbon—for FATHER
1 piece of petit point in hoops—for VINNIE
Yarn, needle and thimble—for VINNIE
1 Bowl for center of table
Supply of artificial fruit for same
1 Flower frog for same
Cigars
Matches (Old-fashioned Parlor matches)
2 Bonnet boxes

108

1 Shirt-waist box
1 Corset box
5 different size packages

Roll of bandage
Roll of adhesive tape—both these
    for HARLAN

PERISHABLES

Bananas—(to fry and use for kip-
    pers)
Oranges
Bacon
Canned apricots (These used for
    scrambled eggs)
Coffee
Tea
Bread
Cake—(Brown and white cakes)
Milk

Sugar
Rice crispies (for oatmeal)
Bottle of burnt sugar for Patent
    medicine
Biscuits
Ladyfinger cake
Cup cake
1 cn. of cinnamon (to be used on
    fried bananas)
Butter

NOTE FOR PROPERTY MAN:

In order to get the best effect of using apricots for scrambled eggs, we
used a number of pieces of toast, cut in squares of about two and a half
inches and made a three-tier pyramid of these in the center of platter
and put apricots on top of toast. The bacon was then put around the
edge of the platter.

In Act III., Scene 1, use fake kippers on platter on table, and one half
of a fried banana on plates of Father and elder boys for eating.

NOTE TO PROPERTY MAN:

The quick changes to and from the breakfast scenes, were made by having
a false table top, the same size as the extended table, already set, off
RIGHT, and carried on by two men and put on table R.C.

The window on the right wall was in a separate flat, hinged to the next
flat upstage. This can be opened during the changes and the fake table
top carried on or off through this opening.

109

NEW PLAYS

★ **THE EXONERATED by Jessica Blank and Erik Jensen.** Six interwoven stories paint a picture of an American criminal justice system gone horribly wrong and six brave souls who persevered to survive it. "The #1 play of the year...intense and deeply affecting..." –*NY Times.* "Riveting. Simple, honest storytelling that demands reflection." –*A.P.* "Artful and moving...pays tribute to the resilience of human hearts and minds." –*Variety.* "Stark...riveting...cunningly orchestrated." –*The New Yorker.* "Hard-hitting, powerful and socially relevant." –*Hollywood Reporter.* [7M, 3W] ISBN: 0-8222-1946-8

★ **STRING FEVER by Jacquelyn Reingold.** Lily juggles the big issues: turning forty, artificial insemination and the elusive scientific Theory of Everything in this Off-Broadway comedy hit. "Applies the elusive rules of string theory to the conundrums of one woman's love life. Think *Sex and the City* meets *Copenhagen*." –*NY Times.* "A funny offbeat and touching look at relationships...an appealing romantic comedy populated by oddball characters." –*NY Daily News.* "Where kooky, zany, and madcap meet...whimsically winsome." –*NY Magazine.* "STRING FEVER will have audience members happily stringing along." –*TheaterMania.com.* "Reingold's language is surprising, inventive, and unique." –*nytheatre.com.* "...[a] whimsical comic voice." –*Time Out.* [3M, 3W (doubling)] ISBN: 0-8222-1952-2

★ **DEBBIE DOES DALLAS adapted by Erica Schmidt, composed by Andrew Sherman, conceived by Susan L. Schwartz.** A modern morality tale told as a comic musical of tragic proportions as the classic film is brought to the stage. "A scream! A saucy, tongue-in-cheek romp." –*The New Yorker.* "Hilarious! DEBBIE manages to have it all: beauty, brains and a great sense of humor!" –*Time Out.* "Shamelessly silly, shrewdly self-aware and proud of being naughty. Great fun!" –*NY Times.* "Racy and raucous, a lighthearted, fast-paced thoroughly engaging and hilarious send-up." –*NY Daily News.* [3M, 5W] ISBN: 0-8222-1955-7

★ **THE MYSTERY PLAYS by Roberto Aguirre-Sacasa.** Two interrelated one acts, loosely based on the tradition of the medieval mystery plays. "... stylish, spine-tingling...Mr. Aguirre-Sacasa uses standard tricks of horror stories, borrowing liberally from masters like Kafka, Lovecraft, Hitchcock...But his mastery of the genre is his own...irresistible." –*NY Times.* "Undaunted by the special-effects limitations of theatre, playwright and *Marvel* comic-book writer Roberto Aguirre-Sacasa maps out some creepy twilight zones in THE MYSTERY PLAYS, an engaging, related pair of one acts...The theatre may rarely deliver shocks equivalent to, say, *Dawn of the Dead*, but Aguirre-Sacasa's work is fine compensation." –*Time Out.* [4M, 2W] ISBN: 0-8222-2038-5

★ **THE JOURNALS OF MIHAIL SEBASTIAN by David Auburn.** This epic one-man play spans eight tumultuous years and opens a uniquely personal window on the Romanian Holocaust and the Second World War. "Powerful." –*NY Times.* "[THE JOURNALS OF MIHAIL SEBASTIAN] allows us to glimpse the idiosyncratic effects of that awful history on one intelligent, pragmatic, recognizably real man..." –*NY Newsday.* [3M, 5W] ISBN: 0-8222-2006-7

★ **LIVING OUT by Lisa Loomer.** The story of the complicated relationship between a Salvadoran nanny and the Anglo lawyer she works for. "A stellar new play. Searingly funny." –*The New Yorker.* "Both generous and merciless, equally enjoyable and disturbing." –*NY Newsday.* "A bitingly funny new comedy. The plight of working mothers is explored from two pointedly contrasting perspectives in this sympathetic, sensitive new play." –*Variety.* [2M, 6W] ISBN: 0-8222-1994-8

DRAMATISTS PLAY SERVICE, INC.
440 Park Avenue South, New York, NY 10016 212-683-8960 Fax 212-213-1539
postmaster@dramatists.com www.dramatists.com

NEW PLAYS

★ **MATCH by Stephen Belber.** Mike and Lisa Davis interview a dancer and choreographer about his life, but it is soon evident that their agenda will either ruin or inspire them—and definitely change their lives forever. "Prolific laughs and ear-to-ear smiles." –*NY Magazine.* "Uproariously funny, deeply moving, enthralling theater. Stephen Belber's MATCH has great beauty and tenderness, and abounds in wit." –*NY Daily News.* "Three and a half out of four stars." –*USA Today.* "A theatrical steeplechase that leads straight from outrageous bitchery to unadorned, heartfelt emotion." –*Wall Street Journal.* [2M, 1W] ISBN: 0-8222-2020-2

★ **HANK WILLIAMS: LOST HIGHWAY by Randal Myler and Mark Harelik.** The story of the beloved and volatile country-music legend Hank Williams, featuring twenty-five of his most unforgettable songs. "[LOST HIGHWAY has] the exhilarating feeling of Williams on stage in a particular place on a particular night…serves up classic country with the edges raw and the energy hot…By the end of the play, you've traveled on a profound emotional journey: LOST HIGHWAY transports its audience and communicates the inspiring message of the beauty and richness of Williams' songs…forceful, clear-eyed, moving, impressive." –*Rolling Stone.* "…honors a very particular musical talent with care and energy… smart, sweet, poignant." –*NY Times.* [7M, 3W] ISBN: 0-8222-1985-9

★ **THE STORY by Tracey Scott Wilson.** An ambitious black newspaper reporter goes against her editor to investigate a murder and finds the *best* story…but at what cost? "A singular new voice…deeply emotional, deeply intellectual, and deeply musical…" –*The New Yorker.* "…a conscientious and absorbing new drama…" –*NY Times.* "…a riveting, tough-minded drama about race, reporting and the truth…" –*A.P.* "… a stylish, attention-holding script that ends on a chilling note that will leave viewers with much to talk about." –*Curtain Up.* [2M, 7W (doubling, flexible casting)] ISBN: 0-8222-1998-0

★ **OUR LADY OF 121st STREET by Stephen Adly Guirgis.** The body of Sister Rose, beloved Harlem nun, has been stolen, reuniting a group of life-challenged childhood friends who square off as they wait for her return. "A scorching and dark new comedy… Mr. Guirgis has one of the finest imaginations for dialogue to come along in years." –*NY Times.* "Stephen Guirgis may be the best playwright in America under forty." –*NY Magazine.* [8M, 4W] ISBN: 0-8222-1965-4

★ **HOLLYWOOD ARMS by Carrie Hamilton and Carol Burnett.** The coming-of-age story of a dreamer who manages to escape her bleak life and follow her romantic ambitions to stardom. Based on Carol Burnett's bestselling autobiography, *One More Time.* "…pure theatre and pure entertainment…" –*Talkin' Broadway.* "…a warm, fuzzy evening of theatre." –*BrodwayBeat.com.* "…chuckles and smiles of recognition or surprise flow naturally…a remarkable slice of life." –*TheatreScene.net.* [5M, 5W, 1 girl] ISBN: 0-8222-1959-X

★ **INVENTING VAN GOGH by Steven Dietz.** A haunting and hallucinatory drama about the making of art, the obsession to create and the fine line that separates truth from myth. "Like a van Gogh painting, Dietz's story is a gorgeous example of excess—one that remakes reality with broad, well-chosen brush strokes. At evening's end, we're left with the author's resounding opinions on art and artifice, and provoked by his constant query into which is greater: van Gogh's art or his violent myth." –*Phoenix New Times.* "Dietz's writing is never simple. It is always brilliant. Shaded, compressed, direct, lucid—he frames his subject with a remarkable understanding of painting as a physical experience." –*Tucson Citizen.* [4M, 1W] ISBN: 0-8222-1954-9

DRAMATISTS PLAY SERVICE, INC.
440 Park Avenue South, New York, NY 10016 212-683-8960 Fax 212-213-1539
postmaster@dramatists.com www.dramatists.com

NEW PLAYS

★ **INTIMATE APPAREL by Lynn Nottage.** The moving and lyrical story of a turn-of-the-century black seamstress whose gifted hands and sewing machine are the tools she uses to fashion her dreams from the whole cloth of her life's experiences. "…Nottage's play has a delicacy and eloquence that seem absolutely right for the time she is depicting…" –*NY Daily News.* "…thoughtful, affecting…The play offers poignant commentary on an era when the cut and color of one's dress—and of course, skin—determined whom one could and could not marry, sleep with, even talk to in public." –*Variety.* [2M, 4W] ISBN: 0-8222-2009-1

★ **BROOKLYN BOY by Donald Margulies.** A witty and insightful look at what happens to a writer when his novel hits the bestseller list. "The characters are beautifully drawn, the dialogue sparkles…" –*nytheatre.com.* "Few playwrights have the mastery to smartly investigate so much through a laugh-out-loud comedy that combines the vintage subject matter of successful writer-returning-to-ethnic-roots with the familiar mid-life crisis." –*Show Business Weekly.* [4M, 3W] ISBN: 0-8222-2074-1

★ **CROWNS by Regina Taylor.** Hats become a springboard for an exploration of black history and identity in this celebratory musical play. "Taylor pulls off a Hat Trick: She scores thrice, turning CROWNS into an artful amalgamation of oral history, fashion show, and musical theater…" –*TheatreMania.com.* "…wholly theatrical…Ms. Taylor has created a show that seems to arise out of spontaneous combustion, as if a bevy of department-store customers simultaneously decided to stage a revival meeting in the changing room." –*NY Times.* [1M, 6W (2 musicians)] ISBN: 0-8222-1963-8

★ **EXITS AND ENTRANCES by Athol Fugard.** The story of a relationship between a young playwright on the threshold of his career and an aging actor who has reached the end of his. "[Fugard] can say more with a single line than most playwrights convey in an entire script…Paraphrasing the title, it's safe to say this drama, making its memorable entrance into our consciousness, is unlikely to exit as long as a theater exists for exceptional work." –*Variety.* "A thought-provoking, elegant and engrossing new play…" –*Hollywood Reporter.* [2M] ISBN: 0-8222-2041-5

★ **BUG by Tracy Letts.** A thriller featuring a pair of star-crossed lovers in an Oklahoma City motel facing a bug invasion, paranoia, conspiracy theories and twisted psychological motives. "…obscenely exciting…top-flight craftsmanship. Buckle up and brace yourself…" –*NY Times.* "…[a] thoroughly outrageous and thoroughly entertaining play…the possibility of enemies, real and imagined, to squash has never been more theatrical." –*A.P.* [3M, 2W] ISBN: 0-8222-2016-4

★ **THOM PAIN (BASED ON NOTHING) by Will Eno.** An ordinary man muses on childhood, yearning, disappointment and loss, as he draws the audience into his last-ditch plea for empathy and enlightenment. "It's one of those treasured nights in the theater—treasured nights anywhere, for that matter—that can leave you both breathless with exhilaration and…in a puddle of tears." –*NY Times.* "Eno's words…are familiar, but proffered in a way that is constantly contradictory to our expectations. Beckett is certainly among his literary ancestors." –*nytheatre.com.* [1M] ISBN: 0-8222-2076-8

★ **THE LONG CHRISTMAS RIDE HOME by Paula Vogel.** Past, present and future collide on a snowy Christmas Eve for a troubled family of five. "…[a] lovely and hauntingly original family drama…a work that breathes so much life into the theater." –*Time Out.* "…[a] delicate visual feast…" –*NY Times.* "…brutal and lovely…the overall effect is magical." –*NY Newsday.* [3M, 3W] ISBN: 0-8222-2003-2

DRAMATISTS PLAY SERVICE, INC.
440 Park Avenue South, New York, NY 10016 212-683-8960 Fax 212-213-1539
postmaster@dramatists.com www.dramatists.com